ARABIC
Dictionary & Phrasebook

English-Arabic
Arabic-English

ARABIC
Dictionary & Phrasebook

English-Arabic
Arabic-English

Mahmoud Gaafar & Jane Wightwick

JAICO PUBLISHING HOUSE
Mumbai • Delhi • Bangalore • Kolkata
Hyderabad • Chennai • Ahmedabad • Bhopal

Published by Jaico Publishing House
121 Mahatma Gandhi Road
Mumbai - 400 023
jaicopub@vsnl.com
www.jaicobooks.com

Published in arrangement with
Hippocrene Books,Inc.
171 Madison Avenue
New York, NY 10016

ARABIC DICTIONARY & PHRASEBOOK
ISBN 81-7992-405-X

First Jaico Impression: 2005

Printed at Efficient Offset Printers, Delhi

CONTENTS

INTRODUCTION

Passport... Ticket... Dictionary & Phrasebook...
Now you're ready for the Middle East!

You probably already know to expect different gestures, sights, smells, customs, body language, and, of course, different sounds. When you first hear people speaking Arabic, you may notice a few sounds that appear to be coming from a mysterious part of their throats. Don't worry, because you are not expected to reproduce these sounds as you read out some phrases to impress your hosts. Do go ahead and try to say some phrases out loud. Remember that meeting a foreigner who is trying to speak Arabic remains pleasantly fascinating to most Arabs, and is usually reason enough for a minor celebration: tea perhaps, or sodas all round.

Spoken Arabic will sound different from one area to the next. At school, however, all Arab children learn the same "Modern Standard Arabic" (MSA). We've tried to use a simplified and functional form of MSA in this book. After all, you just want to get by on your trip and be understood in as many areas as possible. In most Arab countries, if you follow the track already beaten by generations of tourists before you, you can expect to come across English quite often. Once you leave it, however, the real excitement begins, and this book will come into its own.

PRONUNCIATION GUIDE

The pronunciation in this phrasebook is designed to be intuitive. It emphasizes simplicity at the expense of the more subtle Arabic sounds, which can only be properly mastered with time and further study. Remember that the most important thing for you is to be understood.

Many Arabic sounds are familiar and similar to their English equivalents – see Arabic Alphabet on page 9. However, there are some unfamiliar sounds that benefit from additional explanation:

Arabic letter	Pronunciation
خ *kh*	throaty **h** as in the Yiddish **ch**utzpah or the Scottish lo**ch**
ث *th*	soft **th** as in **th**in, often pronounced as **t** or **s** in colloquial dialects
ذ *dh*	hard **th** as in **th**at, often pronounced as **z** in colloquial dialects
غ *gh*	throaty **r** as in the French **r**ue
ح *H*	breathy **h**, as if breathing on glasses to clean them

continued

Arabic letter	Pronunciation
ج *j*	soft **j** as in the French **je**. Pronounced **g** as in **g**ate in Northern Egypt
ص *S*	emphatic **s** (pronounced with the tongue touching the roof the mouth)
ض *D*	emphatic **d**
ط *T*	emphatic **t**
ظ *DH*	emphatic **dh**, often pronounced as an emphatic **d** in colloquial dialects
ع *'*	the letter *'ain* (ع) is difficult for beginners to reproduce. It is a strangulated **ah** sound. We have not rendered the *'ain* directly in the pronunciation, but used an aprostophe ('). To achieve basic communication in Arabic, it is not necessary to reproduce the *'ain*. The context of the sentence will help you to be understood.

THE ARABIC ALPHABET

Opposite you will find the Arabic letters in alphabetical order. The script is written from *right to left* and most Arabic letters join to the following letter in a word. This usually affects the shape of the letter. The chart shows how the letters look at the beginning, in the middle, and at the end of a word.

letter sound	beginning	middle	end
alif a/u/i/aa	ا	ا	ا
baa b	بـ	ـبـ	ب
taa t	تـ	ـتـ	ت
thaa th	ثـ	ـثـ	ث
jaa j	جـ	ـجـ	ج
Haa H	حـ	ـحـ	ح
khaa kh	خـ	ـخـ	خ
daal d	د	د	د
dhaal dh	ذ	ذ	ذ
raa r	ر	ر	ر
zaa z	ز	ز	ز
seen s	سـ	ـسـ	س
sheen sh	شـ	ـشـ	ش
Saad S	صـ	ـصـ	ص
Daad D	ضـ	ـضـ	ض
Taa T	طـ	ـطـ	ط
DHaa DH	ظـ	ـظـ	ظ
'ain '	عـ	ـعـ	ع/ع
ghain gh	غـ	ـغـ	غ/غ
faa f	فـ	ـفـ	ف
qaaf q	قـ	ـقـ	ق
kaaf k	كـ	ـكـ	ك
laam l	لـ	ـلـ	ل
meem m	مـ	ـمـ	م
noon n	نـ	ـنـ	ن
haa h	هـ	ـهـ	ـه/ه
waaw w/oo	و	و	و
yaa y/ee	يـ	ـيـ	ي

ABBREVIATIONS

adj	*adjective*
adv	*adverb*
coll	*colloquial*
fem	*feminine*
masc	*masculine*
n	*noun*
pl	*plural*
pron	*pronoun*
v	*verb*

A BRIEF GRAMMAR

Roots

The Arabic language works around a system of "roots." The root of a word consists of three consonants (non-vowels) that convey a particular concept. For example, the root **d/r/s** carries the concept of "study." This root is manipulated and put into different patterns to create words with related meanings, for example, **daras** *(he studied)*; **diraasa** *(a study)*; **madrasa** *(a school)*; **dars** *(a lesson)*; **mudarris** *(a teacher)*, and so on.

Look out for these roots in words as they could help you remember vocabulary or guess at unknown words.

Genders and Articles

Arabic has two genders: masculine and feminine. Everything you'll meet is either a *he* or a *she*, nothing is an *it*.

Feminine nouns are words that either refer to females, or words that end in **-a** (ة), e.g. بنت **bint** *(girl)*; مدرسة **madrasa** *(school)*; غرفة **ghurfa** *(room)*.

Almost all other nouns are masculine, e.g. ولد **walad** *(boy)*; درس **dars** *(lesson)*; صابون **Saboon** *(soap)*. Exceptions are rare.

There is no indefinite article *(a/an)* in Arabic. ولد **walad** means both *"boy"* and *"a boy."*

The definite article *(the)* is **al-** (الـ), which is added to the beginning of nouns:

ولد **walad** *(a boy)* → الولد **al-walad** *(the boy)*

بنت **bint** *(a girl)* → البنت **al-bint** *(the girl)*

If a noun begins with certain letters of the alphabet, these letters take over (assimilate) the **l** sound of **al-**:

صابون **Saboon** *(soap)* becomes...

الصابون **aS-Saboon** *(the soap)*

درس **dars** *(lesson)* becomes...

الدرس **ad-dars** *(the lesson)*

This assimilation applies to approximately half the letters of the alphabet, but is something you need only to recognize.

If **al-** comes after a word ending in a vowel, the **a** is dropped:

الولد **al-walad** *(the boy)*

هذا الولد **haadha l-walad** *(this boy)*

المتحف **al-matHaf** *(the museum)*

في المتحف **fi l-matHaf** *(in the museum)*

Personal Pronouns

The personal pronouns in Arabic are:

Arabic	English
أنا **ana**	I
أنت **anta**	you (masc)
أنت **anti**	you (fem)
هو **huwa**	he
هي **hiya**	she
نحن **naHnu**	we
أنتم **antum**	you (pl)
هم **hum**	they

Possessive pronouns (my, your, etc.) are added to the end of words:

Ending	Example	Translation
ي **-ee**	كتابي **kitaabee**	my book
ـك **-ak**	كتابك **kitaabak**	your (masc) book
ـك **-ik**	كتابك **kitaabik**	your (fem) book
ـه **-uh**	كتابه **kitaabuh**	his book
ـها **-haa**	كتابها **kitaabhaa**	her book
ـنا **-na**	كتابنا **kitaabna**	our book
ـكم **-kum**	كتابكم **kitaabkum**	your (pl) book
ـهم **-hum**	كتابهم **kitaabhum**	their book

Simple sentences and questions

There is no verb "to be" (am/are/is) in Arabic and no special question form. This means you can make simple statements and questions without using complicated structures. Here are some examples:

Arabic	English
أنا ادوارد. ana Edward	I [am] Edward.
أنا أمريكي. ana amreekeyy	I [am an] American.
أنتم طلبة؟ antum Talaba	[Are] you (pl.) students?
أين المتحف؟ aina l-matHaf	Where [is] the museum?
البنت طويلة. al-bint Taweela	The girl [is] tall.

Adjectives

Adjectives come *after* the word they are describing and will also have **al-** if the word described does:

ولد طويل **walad Taweel** (a tall boy)

المتحف المصري **al-matHaf al-miSreyy**
(the Egyptian Museum)

Adjectives will also have the feminine ending **-a** if the word they describe is feminine:

بنت طويلة **bint Taweela** (a tall girl)

الغرفة الكبيرة **al-ghurfa l-kabeera** (the big room)

Notice the difference between the previous two phrases and the following sentences:

البنت طويلة. **al-bint Taweela** *(The girl [is] tall.)*

الغرفة كبيرة. **al-ghurfa kabeera** *(The room [is] big.)*

Because there is no verb "to be" in Arabic, the difference in meaning is determined only by where you put the article **al-**.

Plurals

Arabic forms the plural in many different ways. The simplest is adding plural endings **-een** or **-aat** to the singular:

Singular	Plural
مدرس **mudarris** *(teacher)*	مدرسين **mudarris<u>een</u>**
اجتماع **ijtimaa'** *(meeting)*	اجتماعات **ijtimaa'<u>aat</u>**

However, many words have plurals that are irregular and need to be learned individually:

Singular	Plural
ولد **walad** *(boy)*	أولاد **awlaad**
بنت **bint** *(girl)*	بنات **banaat**
غرفة **ghurfa** *(room)*	غرف **ghuraf**
كتاب **kitaab** *(book)*	كتب **kutub**

The dictionary section of this book gives the plural of common words after the singular.

Verbs

Arabic has only two tenses: the *present/ future* and the *past*. The person carrying out the action (*I, you, he, she, it,* etc.) is shown by the addition of different endings and prefixes around a stem.

Here is the regular verb **yaktub** *(to write)*. The endings and prefixes are underscored:

Pronoun	Present/future	Past
ana *(I)*	**aktub** أكتب	**katabt** كتبت
anta *(you, masc.)*	**taktub** تكتب	**katabt** كتبت
anti *(you, fem.)*	**taktubeen** تكتبين	**katabt** كتبت
huwa *(he)*	**yaktub** يكتب	**katab** كتب
hiya *(she)*	**taktub** تكتب	**katabat** كتبت
naHnu *(we)*	**naktub** نكتب	**katabna** كتبنا
antum *(you, pl.)*	**taktuboon** تكتبون	**katabtum** كتبتم
hum *(they)*	**yaktuboon** يكتبون	**kataboo** كتبوا

To show that something will take place in the future, **sa-** is sometimes added before the present/future tense:

سنكتب **sa-naktub** *(we will write)*

It is not usually necessary to use a pronoun *(I, you,* etc.) with the verb as the ending shows who is carrying out the action:

درسنا الانجليزية في المدرسة.
darasna l-ingileezey-ya fi l-madrasa
(We studied English in school.)

كتبت رسالة لأمي. **katabt risaala li-ummee**
(I wrote a letter to my mother.)

كل يوم يلعبون التنس. **kull yawm yal'aboon at-tennis**
(Every day they play tennis.)

Verbs are shown in the dictionary under the present tense, third person masculine ("he" form), e.g. **yaktub, yadrus**.

ENGLISH–ARABIC DICTIONARY

A

abbey	دير	dair, adyira
able	قدير	qadeer
above	أعلى	a'laa
absent	غائب	ghaa'ib
accent (n, speech)	لهجة	lahja, lahjaat
accept	يقبل	yaqbal
accident	حادث	Haadith, Hawaadith
accomodation	إقامة	iqaama
account (n, bank)	حساب	Hisaab, Hisaabaat
accountant	محاسب	muHaasib, muHaasibeen
ache (n)	ألم	alam, aalaam
acidity	حموضة	HumooDa
across	بالعرض	bil'arD
activity	نشاط	nashaaT, anshiTa
add	يضيف	yuDeef
address (n, street)	عنوان	'unwaan, 'anaaween
adjust	يعدل	yu'ad-dil
administration	إدارة	idaara
adolescent	مراهق	muraahiq, muraahiqeen
adult	راشد	raashid, raashideen
advanced (adj)	متقدم	mutaqad-dim
adventure	مغامرة	mughaamara, mughaamaraat
advertising (n)	إعلان	i'laan
advice (n)	نصيحة	naSeeHa, naSaa'iH
Afghan (adj)	أفغاني	afghaaneyy, afghaan
Afghanistan	أفغانستان	afghaanistaan
afraid	خائف	khaa'if
after (prep)	بعد	ba'd
afternoon (n)	بعد الظهر	ba'd aDH-DHuhr
again	مرة أخرى	marra ukhra
against	ضد	Didd

age (n)	سن	sinn
agency (n)	وكالة	wikaala, wikaalaat
agree	يوافق	yuwaafiq
agriculture (n)	زراعة	ziraa'a
air (n)	هواء	hawaa'
air conditioning (n)	تكييف الهواء	takyeef al-hawaa'
airmail (n)	بريد جوي	bareed jaw-weyy
airplane	طائرة	Taa'ira, Taa'iraat
airport	مطار	maTaar, maTaaraat
alcohol	الكحول	al-kuHool
Algeria	الجزائر	al-jazaa'ir
Algerian	جزائري	jazaa'ireyy, jazaa'irey-yeen
alive	حي	Hayy
all	كل	kull
Allah	الله	al-laah
allergic	حساس	Has-saas
allow	يسمح	yasmaH
almonds	لوز	lawz
almost	تقريبا	taqreeban
alone	منفرد	munfarid
also	أيضا	aiDan
altitude	ارتفاع	irtifaa', irtifaa'aat
always	دائما	daa'iman
ambassador	سفير	safeer, sufaraa'
amber	كهرمان	kahramaan
ambergris	عنبر	'anbar
ambulance	إسعاف	is'aaf
america	أمريكا	amreeka
american	أمريكي	amreekeyy
amicable	ودي	wid-deyy
amid	وسط	wasT
amount (n)	كمية	kam-mey-ya, kam-mey-yaat
amphitheater	مدرج	mudar-raj
ancestors	أسلاف	aslaaf
ancient	عتيق	'ateeq
angle (n)	زاوية	zaawiya, zawaayaa
angry	غاضب	ghaaDib

animal	حيوان	Hayawaan, Hayawaanaat
another	آخر	aakhar
answer (n)	إجابة	ijaaba, ijaabaat
antiques	تحف قديمة	tuHaf qadeema
antiseptic (adj)	مطهر	muTah-hir
anybody	أي شخص	ayy shakhS
anything	أي شيء	ayy shai'
anywhere	أي مكان	ayy makaan
apartment	شقة	shiq-qa, shuqaq
apologize	يعتذر	ya'tadhir
appetizers	فواتح الشهية	fawaatiH ash-shahey-ya
apple	تفاحة	tufaaHa, tufaaH
appliance	جهاز	jihaaz, ajhiza
appointment	موعد	maw'id, mawaa'eed
apricot	مشمش	mishmish
Arab (adj)	عربي	'arabeyy
Arabic (language)	العربية	al-'arabeyya
architect	معماري (مهندس)	mi'maareyy
arm (n, anatomical)	ذراع	dhiraa'
around	حول	Hawl
arrange	يرتب	yurat-tib
arrival	وصول	wuSool
art	فن	fann
artery	شريان	shiryaan, sharaayeen
artichoke	خرشوف	kharshoof (coll.)
artificial	اصطناعي	iSTinaa'eyy
artist	فنان	fannaan, fannaaneen
ask	يسأل	yas'al
asleep	نائم	naa'im
assist	يعاون	yu'aawin
assortment	تشكيلة	tashkeela
asthma	ربو	rabu
astronomical	فلكي	falakeyy
athletic	رياضي	riyaaDeyy
attorney	محام	muHaami, muHaami-yeen
attractive	جذاب	jadh-dhaab
auction (n)	مزاد	mazaad, mazaadaat

aunt (maternal)	خالة	khaala, khaalaat
aunt (paternal)	عمة	'am-ma, am-maat
authentic	أصلي	aSleyy
author (n)	مؤلف	mu'al-lif, mu'al-lifeen
available	متوفر	mutawaf-fir
average	متوسط	mutawas-siT
azure	أزرق سماوي	azraq samaaweyy

B

Babylon	بابل	baabil
bachelor	أعزب	a'zab, 'uzaab
back (adj, rear)	خلفي	khalfeyy
back (n, anatomical)	ظهر	DHahr, DHuhoor
back (v, support)	يساند	yusaanid
backgammon	طاولة الزهر	Tawlit az-zahr
bad (rotten)	فاسد	faasid
bag (n)	حقيبة	Haqeeba, Haqaa'ib
baggage (n)	أمتعة	amti'a
Bahrain	البحرين	al-baHrayn
Bahraini	بحريني	baHrayneyy
bakery	مخبز	makhbaz, makhaabiz
balance (n, scales)	ميزان	meezaan
balcony	شرفة	shurfa, shurfaat
bald	أصلع	aSla'
ball (n)	كرة	kura, kuraat
bamboo (n)	خيزران	khaizaraan
banana	موزة	mawza, mawz
bangle	خلخال	khal-khaal, khalaa-kheel
barber	حلاق	Hal-laaq, Hal-laaqeen
bargain (n)	صفقة	Safqa, Safqaat
base (n, foundation)	أساس	asaas
basil	ريحان	reeHaan
basket	سلة	sal-la
bathroom	حمام	Ham-maam
bay	شرم	sharm
bay leaves	ورق الغار	waraq al-ghaar

beach	شاطئ	shaaTi', shawaaTi'
beans (fava)	فول	fool
beans (green)	فاصوليا	faSolya
beans (runner)	لوبيا	lubya
beard	لحية	liHya, liHaa
beat (n, tempo, music)	إيقاع	eeqaa'
beat (v, hit)	يضرب	yaDrib
beaten (adj, whisked)	مخفوق	makhfooq
beautiful	جميل	jameel
because	لأن	la'ann
become	يصبح	yuSbiH
bed	سرير	sareer, asir-ra
bedouin	بدوي	badaweyy
bedroom	غرفة نوم	ghurfat nawm
bee	نحلة	naHla, naHl
beech (wood)	خشب الزان	khashab az-zaan
beef	لحم بقري	laHm baqareyy
beer	بيرة	beera
before	قبل	qabl
begin	يبدأ	yabda'
behind	خلف	khalf
belief	إيمان	eemaan
believe	يصدق	yuSad-diq
below	أسفل	asfal
bend (n, contour)	انحناء	inHinaa'
benefit (n)	فائدة	faa'ida, fawaa'id
Berber	بربر	barbar
beside	بجانب	bijaanib
best (adj & n)	أحسن	aHsan
bet (n)	رهان	rahaan, rahaanaat
Bethlehem	بيت لحم	bait laHm
better (adj & n)	أفضل	afDal
between	بين	bain
beyond	ما وراء	maa waraa'
bible	انجيل	injeel
bicycle	دراجة	dar-raaja, dar-raajaat
big	كبير	kabeer

bilingual	بلغتين	bilughatain
bird	طائر	Taa'ir, Tiyoor
birth (n)	ولادة	wilaada, wilaadaat
birthday	عيد ميلاد	'eed milaad
black (color)	أسود	aswad
black coffee (no sugar)	قهوة سادة	qahwa saada
bladder	مثانة	mathaana
blank	فارغ	faarigh
blanket	بطانية	baT-Taney-ya, baTaaTeen
bleed	ينزف	yanzif
blend (n, mix)	خليط	khaleeT
blind (adj, without sight)	أعمى	a'maa
blonde (adj)	أشقر	ashqar
blood (n)	دم	dam
blood group	فصيلة الدم	faSeelat ad-dam
blood test	فحص دم	faHS dam
blood transfusion	نقل دم	naql dam
blouse	بلوزة	bilooza
blue	أزرق	azraq
boat	مركب	markib, maraakib
body	جسم	jism, ajsaam
boil (v, heat)	يغلي	yaghlee
bone	عظمة	'aDHma, 'iDHaam
book (n, novel, etc.)	كتاب	kitaab, kutub
book (v, reserve)	يحجز	yaHjiz
bookshop	مكتبة	maktaba, maktabaat
boring (adj, tedious)	ممل	mumill
bottle (n, glass container)	زجاجة	zujaaja, zujaajaat
box (n)	علبة	'ulba, 'ulab
boy	ولد	walad, awlaad
bracelet	سوار	siwaar
brain	مخ	mukh
brakes	مكابح	makaabiH
brass	نحاس أصفر	naHaas aSfar
bread	خبز	khubz
break (n, respite)	استراحة	istiraaHa
break (v, smash)	يكسر	yaksir

breakdown (itemization)	بيان مفصل	bayaan mufaS-Sal
breakdown (malfunction)	تعطل	Ta'aT-Tul
breakdown (nervous)	انهيار عصبي	inhiyaar 'aSabeyy
breakfast	فطور	fuToor
breast	صدر	Sadr, Sudoor
breed (n)	سلالة	sulaala, sulaalaat
breed (v)	يربي	yurab-bi
bride	عروسة	'aroosa, 'araa'is
bridegroom	عريس	'arees, 'irsaan
bridge (n)	جسر	jisr, jusoor
Britain	بريطانيا	biriTaanya
British (adj)	بريطاني	biriTaaneyy, biriTaaney-yeen
broker	سمسار	simsaar, samaasira
brother	أخ	akh, ukhwa
brown	بني	bun-neyy
budget (adj, cheap)	اقتصادي	iqtiSaadeyy
budget (n, fiscal framework)	ميزانية	meezaney-ya
buffalo	جاموسة	jaamoosa, jaamoos
building	بناء	binaa', abneya
bureau de change	مكتب صراف	maktab Sar-raaf
bureaucracy	بيروقراطية	beeroqraTey-ya
burglary	سرقة	sariqa, sariqaat
burn (v)	يحرق	yaHriq
burst (v)	ينفجر	yan-fajir
bus	باص	baaS, baaSaat
busy (adj)	مشغول	mash-ghool
butcher (n)	جزار	jaz-zaar, jaz-zaareen
butter	زبد	zubd
button (n)	زر	zirr
buy (v)	يشتري	yashtaree

C

cab (n)	تاكسي	taksee
cabin (n)	كابينة	kabeena, kabaa'in

cable (n)	سلك	silk, aslaak
cactus	صبار	Sab-baar
Cairo	القاهرة	al-qaahira
calculate	يحسب	yaHsib
caliph	خليفة	khaleefa, kholafaa'
call (n, a phonecall)	مكالمة	mukaalama, mukaalamaat
call (v, phone someone)	يتصل	yat-taS-Sil
call (v, summon)	ينادي	yunaadi
calligraphy	فن الخط	fann al-khaTT
calm (adj)	ساكن	saakin
camel	جمل	jamal, jimaal
camping trip (n)	التخييم	at-takhyeem
canal (n, channel)	قناة	qanaah, qanawaat
cancellation	إلغاء	ilghaa'
candle	شمعة	sham'a, shimoo'
candy	حلوى	Halwaa
canvas	خيش	khaish
capital (city)	عاصمة	'aaSima, 'awaaSim
car	سيارة	say-yaara, say-yaaraat
carafe	دورق	dawraq, dawaariq
card	بطاقة	biTaaqa, biTaaqaat
cardamom	حبهان	Hab-bahaan
care (n)	عناية	'inaaya
carelessness (n)	إهمال	ihmaal
carnation	قرنفل	qaranful
carnelian	عقيق أحمر	'aqeeq aHmar
carpenter	نجار	naj-jaar, naj-jaareen
carpet (n)	سجادة	sij-jaada, sij-jaad
carrot	جزر	jazar
carry (v)	يحمل	yaHmil
Casablanca	الدار البيضاء	ad-daar al- bayDaa'
case (n, court)	قضية	qaDey-ya
case (n, instance)	حالة	Haala
case (n, pillow)	كيس وسادة	kees wisaada
castle	قلعة	qal'a, qilaa'
cat	قطة	qiT-Ta, qiTaT
catacomb	سرداب	sirdaab, saraadeeb

catch (v, hold)	يمسك	yamsik
catch (v, fish, etc.)	يصطاد	yaSTaad
cause (n, reason)	سبب	sabab, asbaab
caution (n, prudence)	احتراس	iHtiraas
caution (n, warning)	تحذير	taHdheer
cave (n)	كهف	kahf, kuhoof
cavity	تجويف	tajweef
cedar (n)	شجرة الأرز	shajarat al-arz
ceiling	سقف	saqf
celebration	احتفال	iHtifaal, iHtifaalaat
celery	كرفس	karafs
central (adj, main)	مركزي	markazeyy
central (adj, middle)	متوسط	muTawas-siT
cereal (breakfast)	حبوب الفطور	Huboob al-fuToor
certainty	يقين	yaqeen
chair	كرسي	kursee, karaasee
chance	صدفة	Sudfa
change (n, alteration)	تغيير	taghyeer, taghyeeraat
change (n, coins)	فكة	fak-ka
change (v, money, etc.)	يغير	yughay-yir
charge (n, accusation)	تهمة	tuhma
charge (n, fee)	أجر	ajr, ujoor
charge (v, fill up)	يشحن	yash-Hin
charge card	بطاقة حساب	biTaaqat Hisaab
charity (n, donation)	صدقة	Sadaqa, Sadaqaat
charity (n, organization)	منظمة خيرية	munaDH-DHama khairey-ya
cheap	رخيص	rakheeS
cheat (v)	يغش	yaghish
check (adj, pattern)	مربعات	murab-ba'aat
check (n, bill)	فاتورة	fatoora, fawaateer
cheese	جبنة	jubna
chemistry	كيمياء	keemyaa'
cherries	كرز	karz
chicken	دجاج	dajaaj
chickpeas	حمص	Hum-muS
child	طفل	Tifl, aTfaal

choice	اختيار	ikhtiyaar
Christian	مسيحي	maseeHeyy, maseeHey-yeen
Christianity	المسيحية	al-maseeHey-ya
chronic	مزمن	muzmin
church	كنيسة	kaneesa, kanaa'is
circle (n)	دائرة	daa'ira, dawaa'ir
circumcision	ختان	khitaan
citadel	قلعة	qal'a, qilaa'
city	مدينة	madeena, mudun
civilization	حضارة	HaDaara, HaDaaraat
clean (adj)	نظيف	naDHeef
clear (adj, unambiguous)	واضح	waaDiH
clear (adj, unclouded)	صاف	Saafi
client	زبون	zuboon, zabaa'in
climb (n)	تسلق	tasal-luq
climb (v)	يتسلق	yatasal-laq
close (adv, near)	قريب	qareeb
closed	مغلق	mughlaq
closet	خزانة ملابس	khazaanat malaabis
clothes	ملابس	malaabis
coach (n, bus)	باص	baaS, baaSaat
coach (n, trainer)	مدرب	mudar-rib, mudar-ribeen
coast (n, shore)	ساحل	saaHil, sawaaHil
coffee (beans)	بن	bunn
coffee (beverage)	قهوة	qahwa
coffee cup reader	قارءة الفنجان	qaari'at al-finjaan
cold (adj)	بارد	baarid
college	كلية	kul-ley-ya, kul-ley-yaat
colloquial language	العامية	al-'aamey-ya
color (n)	لون	lawn, alwaan
come (v)	يأتي	ya'tee
comfortable	مريح	mureeH
commercial district	حي تجاري	Hayy tijaareyy
commission (n, percentage fee)	عمولة	'umoola, 'umoolaat
common (adj, familiar)	مألوف	ma'loof
companion	رفيق	rafeeq, rifaaq

company (n, business)	شركة	sharika, sharikaat
company (n, guests)	ضيوف	Duyoof
compensation	تعويض	ta'weeD
complain	يشكو	yashkoo
complement (v, make whole)	يكمل	yukam-mil
compliment (v)	يمدح	yamdaH
complimentary	مجاني	maj-jaaneyy
compromise (n)	حل وسط	Hall wasaT
compulsory	اجباري	ijbaari
concerned (worried)	قلق	qaliq
concert (n)	حفلة موسيقية	Hafla museeqey-ya
concussion	ارتجاج	irtijaaj
condition (n, state)	حالة	Haala
condition (n, stipulation)	شرط	sharT, shurooT
condom	عازل طبي	'aazil Tib-beyy, 'awaazil Tib-bey-ya
confirm	يؤكد	yu'ak-kid
connect	يوصل	yawSil
consent (n)	تراض	taraaDi
constant	دائم	daa'im
constipation	إمساك	imsaak
construct	يشيد	yushay-yid
consulate	قنصلية	qunSuley-ya, qunSuley-yaat
consultant	استشاري	istishaareyy
contagious	معد	mu'di
contradictory	متناقض	mutanaaqiD
convenient	مناسب	munaasib
cook (n, chef)	طباخ	Tab-baakh, Tab-baakheen
cook (v)	يطبخ	yaTbukh
Copt (n)	قبطي	qibTeyy, aqbaaT
coral	شعاب مرجانية	shi'aab marjaaney-ya
corner (n)	ركن	rukn, arkaan
cost (n)	ثمن	thaman
cotton (n)	قطن	quTn
cough (n)	سعال	su'aal
count (v, compute)	يعد	ya'idd

country (n, state)	دولة	*dawla*
countryside	ريف	*reef*
couple	اثنين	*ithnain*
cousin (daughter of maternal aunt)	بنت خالة	*bint khaala, banaat khaala*
cousin (daughter of maternal uncle)	بنت خال	*bint khaal, banaat khaal*
cousin (daughter of paternal aunt)	بنت عمة	*bint 'amma, banaat 'amma*
cousin (daughter of paternal uncle)	بنت عم	*bint 'amm, banaat 'amm*
cousin (son of maternal aunt)	ابن خالة	*ibn khaala, abnaa' khaala*
cousin (son of maternal uncle)	ابن خال	*ibn khaal, abnaa' khaal*
cousin (son of paternal aunt)	ابن عمة	*ibn 'amma, abnaa' 'amma*
cousin (son of paternal uncle)	ابن عم	*ibn 'amm, abnaa' 'amm*
cover (n, lid)	غطاء	*ghaTaa', aghTey-ya*
cover (v)	يغطئ	*yughaTTi'*
coverage (n, insurance)	تأمين	*ta'meen*
cow	بقرة	*baqara, baqar*
craftsmanship	حرفية	*Hirafey-ya*
crash (n)	تصادم	*taSaadum*
crazy	مخبول	*makhbool*
creativity	ابتكار	*ibtikaar*
credit (n)	ضمان	*Damaan*
crescent	هلال	*hilaal*
crime	جريمة	*jareema, jaraa'im*
criminal (n)	مجرم	*mujrim, mujrimeen*
critical (adj, dangerous)	خطير	*khaTeer*
crocodile	تمساح	*timsaaH, tamaaseeH*
crook	نصاب	*naS-Saab, naS-Saabeen*
cross (adj, angry)	غضبان	*ghaDbaan*
cross (n, crucifix)	صليب	*Saleeb*
cross (v, interbreed)	يهجن	*yahaj-jin*

cross (v, movement)	يعبر	ya'bur
cruise (n)	جولة بحرية	jawla baHrey-ya
crushed (adj, powdered)	مسحوق	masHooq
cry (v, weep)	يبكي	yabkee
cry (v, yell)	يصرخ	yaSrukh
cucumber	خيار	khiyaar
cul-de-sac	طريق مسدود	Tareeq masdood
cultured (erudite)	مثقف	muthaq-qaf, muthaq-qafeen
cup (n, for drinks)	فنجان	finjaan, fanajeen
cup (n, trophy)	كأس	ka's, ku'oos
cure (n, treatment)	علاج	'ilaaj
currency	عملة	'umla, 'umlaat
current (n, electric)	تيار كهربائي	tay-yaar kahrubaa'eyy
current (n, water)	تيار مائي	tay-yaar maa'eyy
current account	حساب جار	Hisaab jaari
current affairs	شؤون الساعة	shu'oon as-saa'a
curse (n, evil spell)	لعنة	la'na
curse (v, abuse verbally)	يشتم	yashtim
curtain	ستار	sitaar
customs (n, import duties)	جمارك	jamaarik
customs (n, traditions)	تقاليد	taqaaleed
cut (v, tear)	يقطع	yaqTa'
cycling	ركوب الدراجات	rukoob ad-dar-raajaat

D

dagger	خنجر	khanjar, khanaajir
daily	يومي	yawmeyy
dairy products	منتجات الألبان	muntajaat al-albaan
dam	سد	sadd, sudood
damage (n)	تلف	talaf
Damascus	دمشق	dimashq
dance (v)	يرقص	yarquS
dangerous	خطر	khaTir
dark (unlit)	مظلم	muDHlim
date (appointment)	موعد	maw'id, mawaa'eed

date (day)	تاريخ	taareekh, tawaareekh
date (fruit)	بلحة	balaHa, balaH
date (tree)	نخلة	nakhla, nakhlaat
daughter	ابنة	ibna, banaat
dawn (n)	فجر	fajr
day	يوم	yawm, ayaam
deadly	مميت	mumeet
deaf	أصم	aSamm
decide	يقرر	yaqar-rir
deduct	يخصم	yakhSim
deep (adj)	عميق	'ameeq
deer	غزال	ghazaal
degree (extent)	درجة	daraja, darajaat
degree (university certificate)	شهادة جامعية	shihaada jaame'ey-ya
delicate	رقيق	raqeeq
deliver	يوصل	yuwaS-Sil
dense	كثيف	katheef
dentist	طبيب أسنان	Tabeeb asnaan
dentures	طقم أسنان	Taqm asnaan
departure	رحيل	raHeel
deport (v)	يطرد	yaTrud
deposit (v, place securely)	يودع	yudi'
dervish	درويش	darweesh, daraaweesh
descendant	سليل	saleel
describe	يصف	vaSif
desert (n)	صحراء	SaHraa'
design (v)	يصمم	yuSam-mim
dessert	طبق الحلو	Tabaq al-Hilw
destination	وجهة	wijha, wijhaat
details	تفاصيل	tafaaSeel
detergent	منظف	munaDH-DHif, munaDH-DHifaat
devil	شيطان	shayTaan, shayaaTeen
diabetes	مرض السكر	maraD as-suk-kar
diagnosis	تشخيص	tash-kheeS

dial (v)	يطلب بالتليفون	*yaTlub bit-tilifoon*
dialect	لهجة	*lahja, lahjaat*
dialing tone	حرارة (تليفون)	*Haraara*
diamonds	ماس	*maas*
diaper	حفاضة	*Haf-faaDa*
diarrhea	إسهال	*is-haal*
dictionary	قاموس	*qaamoos, qawaamees*
diet	نظام تغذية	*niDHaam tagh-dheya*
difference	فرق	*farq, furooq*
difficult	صعب	*Sa'b*
dinner	عشاء	*'ashaa'*
direct (adj, non-stop)	مباشر	*mubaashir*
direct (v, a movie, etc.)	يخرج	*yukhrij*
direct (v, give directions)	يدل	*yadull*
director (n, executive)	مدير	*mudeer*
dirty (adj)	قذر	*qadhir*
disability	عجز	*'ajz*
disabled (n)	معاق	*mu'aaq*
discount (n)	خصم	*khaSm, khuSumaat*
disease	مرض	*maraD, amraaD*
dish (n)	طبق	*Tabaq, aTbaaq*
dishwasher	غسالة أطباق	*ghas-saalat aTbaaq*
disinfect	يطهر	*yuTah-hir*
dissolve	يذوب	*yudhoob*
distance (n)	مسافة	*masaafa*
divide (v)	يقسم	*yuqas-sim*
diving (n, scuba)	غوص	*ghawS*
divorce (n)	طلاق	*Talaaq*
dog	كلب	*kalb, kilaab*
doll	دمية	*dumya, dumyaat*
dolphin	درفيل	*darfeel, daraafeel*
dome	قبة	*qub-ba, qibaab*
donkey	حمار	*Himaar, Hameer*
door	باب	*baab, abwaab*
doorbell	جرس الباب	*jaras al-baab*
dosage	جرعة	*jur'a, jur'aat*
double (adj)	مزدوج	*muzdawaj*

doubt (n)	شك	shakk
dough	عجين	'ajeen
down (n, feathers)	زغب	zaghab
down payment	مقدم	muqad-dam
down river	مع مجرى النهر	ma' majraa an-nahr
down(wards)	إلى أسفل	ila asfal
dozen	دستة	dasta
draw (v, attract)	يجذب	yajdhub
draw (v, illustrate)	يرسم	yarsim
draw (v, pull behind)	يجر	yajurr
dream (n)	حلم	Hilm, aHlaam
dream (v)	يحلم	yaHlam
dress (n, clothing item)	فستان	fustaan, fasaateen
dressing (n, salad flavoring)	توابل السلطة	tawaabil as-salaTa
drink (n)	مشروب	mashroob, mashroobaat
drink (v)	يشرب	yashrib
driver	سائق	saa'iq, saa'iqeen
drown	يغرق	yaghriq
drug (medication)	دواء	dawaa', adweya
drug (narcotic)	مخدر	mukhad-dir, mukhad-diraat
drugstore	صيدلية	Saydaley-ya, Saydaley-yaat
dry (adj)	جاف	jaaf
duck (n)	بطة	baT-Ta, baTT
during (prep)	خلال	khilaal
dust (n)	تراب	turaab
duty (n, obligation)	واجب	waajib, waajibaat
duty (n, tax)	ضريبة	Dareeba, Daraa'ib
dye (v)	يصبغ	yaSbigh
dynasty (n)	أسرة حاكمة	usra Haakima

E

each	كل	kull
eagle	نسر	nisr, nisoor
ear	أذن	udhun, aadhaan
early	مبكر	mubak-kir

earth (planet)	الكرة الأرضية	al-kura l-arDey-ya
east (n)	شرق	sharq
Easter	عيد الفصح	eed al-fiSH
eastern	شرقي	sharqeyy, sharqey-yeen
eat	ياكل	ya'kul
economic	اقتصادي	iqtiSaadeyy
edge	حد	Hadd, Hudood
education	تعليم	ta'leem
effective	فعال	fa'aal
effort	جهد	juhd, juhood
egg	بيضة	baiDa, baiD
eggplant	باذنجان	baadhinjaan
Egypt	مصر	miSr
Egyptian	مصري	misreyy, miSrey-yeen
Egyptology	علم المصريات	'ilm al-miSrey-yaat
elbow	كوع	koo', akwaa'
elder (n)	الأكبر	al-akbar
elderly (adj)	مسن	musinn, musin-neen
electricity	كهرباء	kahrabaa'
elementary (basic)	أساسي	asaaseyy
elephant	فيل	feel, afyaal
elevator	مصعد	miS'ad, maSaa'id
else	آخر	aakhar
embalming (n)	تحنيط	taHneeT
embassy	سفارة	sifaara, sifaaraat
embroidered	مطرز	moTar-raz
emerald (n)	زمرد	zumur-rud
emergency (n)	طوارئ	Tawaari'
emir	أمير	ameer, umaraa'
Emirates	الإمارات	al-imaaraat
employee	موظف	muwaDH-DHaf, muwaDH-DHafeen
empty	فارغ	faarigh
end (n)	نهاية	nihaaya
energetic	نشيط	nasheeT
engagement (n, appointment)	ارتباط	irtibaaT, irtibaaTaat

engagement (n, for marriage)	خطوبة	khuTooba
engine	محرك	muHar-rik, muHar-rikaat
engineer	مهندس	muhandis, muhandiseen
England	انجلترا	ingeltera
English (language)	اللغة الانجليزية	al-lugha al-ingeleezey-ya
English (person)	انجليزي	ingeleezeyy, ingeleez
engraved (adj)	منقوش	manqoosh
enjoy	يستمتع	yastamti'
enough	كفاية	kifaaya
enter	يدخل	yadkhol
entertainment	تسلية	tasliya
entrance	مدخل	madkhal, madaakhil
envelope	مظروف	maDHroof, maDHaareef
environment	بيئة	bee'a
epilepsy (n)	صرع	Sara'
equal (adj)	مساو	musawi
equestrian (adj)	خاص بالفروسية	khaaS bil-furoosey-ya
error	خطأ	khaTa', akhTaa'
escape (v)	يهرب	yahrab
essential	ضروري	Darooreyy
estimate (n)	تقدير	taqdeer
estimate (v)	يقدر	yuqad-dir
Euphrates	الفرات	al-furaat
Euro	اليورو	al-yooroo
Europe	أوروبا	orob-baa
European	أوروبي	orob-beyy, orob-bey-yeen
even (adj, leveled)	متساو	mutasaawi
evening	مساء	masaa'
ever (adv)	أبدا	abadan
every	كل	kull
exact	مضبوط	maDbooT
examination (n, medical)	فحص	faHS, fuHooSaat
examination (n, school)	امتحان	imtiHaan, imtiHaanaat
example	مثال	mithaal, amthila
excavation	تنقيب	tanqeeb
exceed	يتجاوز	yatajaawaz

excellence	امتياز	imtiyaaz
except	ما عدا	maa 'adaa
exchange (n)	مبادلة	mubaadala
exchange (v)	يبادل	yubaadil
excursion	جولة	jawla, jawlaat
excuse (n)	عذر	'udhr, a'dhaar
exempt	معفي	ma'fi
exercise (n)	تمرين	tamreen, tamreenaat
exhaust (n, fumes)	عادم	'aadim
exhausted	مرهق	murhaq
exhibition	معرض	maa'riD, ma'aariD
exit (n)	مخرج	makhraj, makhaarij
expect	يتوقع	yatawaq-qa'
expenses	مصاريف	maSaareef
expensive	غال	ghali
experience (n)	خبرة	khibra, khibraat
expiration date	تاريخ انتهاء الصلاحية	tareekh intihaa' aS-SalaaHiya
explain	يشرح	yashraH
explore	يستكشف	yastakshif
expression (phrase)	تعبير	ta'beer, ta'beeraat
exterior	خارجي	khaarijeyy
extinguish	يطفئ	yuTfi'
extra	إضافي	iDaafeyy
extraction (n, tooth, etc.)	خلع	khal'
eye (n, anatomical)	عين	'ain, 'uyoon
eyebrow	حاجب	Haajib, Hawaajib
eyelash	رمش	rimsh, rumoosh
eyesight	بصر	baSar

F

fabric	قماش	qumaash, aqmisha
face (n, anatomy)	وجه	wajh, wujooh
fact	حقيقة	Haqeeqa, Haqaa'iq
factory	مصنع	maSna', maSaani'
faint (v, pass out)	يغمى عليه	yughma 'alaih

fair (just)	عادل	'aadil
faith	إيمان	'eeman
faithful (adj)	وفي	wafeyy
fake (adj)	مزيف	muzayyaf
falcon	صقر	Saqr, Suqoor
fall (n, season)	الخريف	al-khareef
fall (v, tumble)	يسقط	yasquT
family	أسرة	usra, usarr
famous	مشهور	mash-hoor
fan (n, cooling)	مروحة	marwaHa, maraawiH
far	بعيد	ba'eed
fare	أجرة	ujra
farm (n)	مزرعة	mazra'a, mazaari'
fashion	موضة	moDa
fast (adj, speedy)	سريع	saree'
fast (n)	صوم	Sawm
fast (v)	يصوم	yaSoom
fat (n)	دهن	duhn
fatal	مميت	mumeet
father (n)	أب	ab
father-in-law	حمو	Hamw
faucet	حنفية	Hanafey-ya, Hanafey-yaat
fault (n)	خلل	khalal
fear (n)	خوف	khawf
fear (v)	يخاف من	yakhaaf min
feast (n)	عيد	'eed, a'yaad
feed (v)	يطعم	yuT'im
feel (v)	يشعر	yash'ur
female	أنثى	untha
ferry (n)	معدية	mi'ad-dey-ya
festival	مهرجان	mahrajaan
fever	حمى	Hum-maa
few (adj)	قليل	qaleel
fez	طربوش	Tarboosh
fiancé (male)	خطيب	khaTeeb
fiancée (female)	خطيبة	khaTeeba
fig	تينة	teena, teen

fight (v)	يقاتل	yuqaatil
fill (v)	يملأ	yamla'
filly	مهرة	muhra
final	نهائي	nihaa'i
find (v)	يجد	yajid
fine (n)	غرامة	gharaama, gharaamaat
finger	إصبع	iSba', aSaabi'
finish (v)	ينهي	yunhee
fire (n, flame)	نار	naar
fire (v, terminate employment)	يفصل	yafSil
first	أول	aw-wal
fish (n)	سمك	samak
fish (v)	يصطاد سمك	yaSTaaD samak
fitting (adj, suitable)	مناسب	munaasib
fitting (n, trying on)	قياس	qiyaas
fix (v)	يصلح	yuSliH
flat (adj, opp. bumpy)	مسطح	musaT-TaH
flavor	مذاق	madhaaq
flight (n, air journey)	رحلة طيران	riHlet Tayaraan
floor (n)	أرضية	arDey-ya
florist	محل ورد	maHall ward
flour	دقيق	daqeeq
flower (n, rose, etc.)	وردة	warda, ward
flush (n)	سيفون	seefon
fly (n, insect)	ذبابة	dhobaaba, dhobaab
fly (n, zipper)	سوستة	sosta, sosat
fly (v)	يطير	yaTeer
fog	ضباب	Dabaab
follow	يتبع	yatba'
food	أكل	akl
foot	قدم	qadam, aqdaam
forbidden	ممنوع	mamnoo'
foreigner	أجنبي	ajnabee
forget	ينسى	yansa
fork	شوكة	shawka, shuwak
formal (adj)	رسمي	rasmee

fortress	قلعة	qal'a, qilaa'
forward (adj)	أمامي	amaameyy
fountain	نافورة	nafoora, nafooraat
fracture (n)	كسر	kasr
fragile	هش	hash-sh
frank (honest)	صريح	SareeH
free (adj, gratis)	مجاني	maj-jaaneyy
fresh	طازج	Taazij
fridge	ثلاجة	thal-laaja, thal-laajaat
friend	صديق	Sadeeq, aSdiqaa'
frozen (adj)	مجمد	mujam-mad
fruit	فاكهة	faakiha, fawaakih
fry	يقلي	yaqlee
fuel (n)	وقود	waqood
full	كامل	kaamil
funny (humorous)	مضحك	muD-Hik
funny (peculiar)	غريب	ghareeb
future (n)	مستقبل	mustaqbal

G

gallant	شهم	shahm
gallery (n, exhibition)	معرض	ma'raD, ma'aariD
gallon	جالون	galoon
gambling	قمار	qumaar
garden	حديقة	Hadeeqa, Hadaa'iq
garlic	ثوم	thawm
gas (n, petrol)	بنزين	banzeen
gastric	معوي	ma'aweyy
gate	بوابة	baw-waaba, baw-waabaat
gazelle	غزال	ghazaal, ghuzlaan
gem	جوهرة	jawhara, jawaahir
generous	كريم	kareem
genuine	أصلي	aSleyy
germs	جراثيم	jaraatheem
gift	هدية	hadey-ya, hadaaya
ginger (n, herb)	جنزبيل	ganzabeel

girl	بنت	*bint, banaat*
give	يعطي	*yu'Tee*
gland	غدة	*ghud-da, ghud-dad*
glass (n, material)	زجاج	*zujaaj*
glass (n, tumbler, etc.)	كوب	*koob, akwaab*
glasses	نظارة	*naDH-DHaara*
go	يذهب	*yadh-hab*
goat	عنزة	*'anza, anzaat*
God	الله	*al-laah*
gold (n)	ذهب	*dhahab*
good	حسن	*Hasan*
gossip (v)	يدردش	*yudardish*
grace (n, elegance)	رشاقة	*rashaaqa*
graduate (adj)	خريج	*khir-reej*
grandchild	حفيد	*Hafeed, aHfaad*
grandfather	جد	*jidd*
grape	عنبة	*'inaba, 'inab*
gratitude (adj)	امتنان	*imtinaan*
gratuity	إكرامية	*ikraamey-ya, ikraamey-yaat*
great (adj, marvelous)	عظيم	*'aDHeem*
greeting (n)	تحية	*taHey-ya, taHey-yaat*
grocer	بقال	*baq-qaal*
group (n)	مجموعة	*majmoo'a, majmoo'aat*
grow	ينمو	*yanmoo*
guard (n)	حارس	*Haaris, Hor-ras*
guardian	وصي	*waSeyy*
guava	جوافة	*jawaafa*
guest (n)	ضيف	*Daif, Duyoof*
guidebook	دليل	*daleel*
gulf	خليج	*khaleej*
gynecology	أمراض نساء	*amraaD nisaa'*

H

habitat	موطن	*mawTin*
haggle (v)	يساوم	*yusaawim*
hair	شعر	*sha'r*

hairdresser	كوافير	*kewafeer*
half	نصف	*niSf, anSaaf*
hall	بهو	*bahw*
hand (n, anatomy)	يد	*yad, ayaadi*
handbag	حقيبة يد	*Haqeebat yad*
handkerchief	منديل	*mindeel*
handsome	وسيم	*waseem*
happen (v)	يحدث	*yaHduth*
happy	سعيد	*sa'eed*
harass	يضايق	*yuDaayiq*
harbor	ميناء	*meena', mawaani'*
harm (n)	ضرر	*Darar*
hat	قبعة	*quba'a*
hate (v)	يكره	*yakrah*
have	يملك	*yamluk*
hawk	صقر	*Saqr, Suqoor*
hazard	خطر	*khaTar*
head (n, anatomy)	رأس	*ra's, ru'oos*
head (v, move towards)	يتجه	*yat-tajih*
headache	صداع	*Sodaa'*
headlights	ضوء عال	*Daw' 'aali*
heal (mend)	يلتئم	*yalta'im*
health	صحة	*SiH-Ha*
heart	قلب	*qalb, quloob*
heat (n)	سخونة	*sukhoona*
heater	مدفأة	*midfa'a*
heavy	ثقيل	*thaqeel*
help (n)	مساعدة	*musaa'ida*
help (v)	يساعد	*yusaa'id*
henna	حناء	*Henaa'*
hepatitis	صفراء	*Safraa'*
herb	عشب	*'ushb, a'shaab*
here	هنا	*huna*
hereditary	وراثي	*wiraathy*
hieroglyphic	هيروغليفي	*heeroghleefee*
high (tall)	عال	*aali*
hill	تل	*tall, tilaal*

hire (v)	يؤجر	yu'aj-jir
history	تاريخ	tareekh
hobby	هواية	huwaaya, huwayaat
hold (v, grip)	يمسك	yamsik
hole	ثقب	thuqb, thuqoob
holiday (n)	عطلة	uTla, uTlaat
holy	مقدس	muqad-das
home (dwelling)	بيت	bait, buyoot
honey	عسل	'asal
hoof	حافر	Haafir, Hawaafir
hookah	شيشة	sheesha
hope (v)	يأمل	ya'mal
hornet	دبور	dab-boor, dabaabeer
horse	حصان	HiSaan, aHSina
hospital	مستشفى	mustashfa
hospitality	كرم الضيافة	karam aD-Diyaafa
hot	حار	Harr
hotel	فندق	funduq, fanaadiq
hotel lobby	صالة الفندق	Saalat al-funduq
hour	ساعة	saa'a, sa'aat
house	دار	daar, diyaar
how	كيف	kaif
humidity	رطوبة	ruTooba
hump (n, camel's back)	سنام	sanaam
hunger (n)	جوع	joo'
hurry (v)	يسرع	yusri'
hurt (v)	يؤلم	yu'lim
husband	زوج	zawj, azwaaj
hypertension	انخفاض ضغط الدم	inkhifaaD Daght ad-dam

I

I	أنا	ana
ice	ثلج	thalj
icon	أيقونة	ayqoona, ayqoonaat
idea	فكرة	fikra, afkaar
identical	مطابق	muTaabiq

if	لو	*lau*
ill (adj, sick)	مريض	*mareeD*
illegal	غير قانوني	*ghair qaanooneyy*
imagine	يتصور	*yataSaw-war*
imitation (adj, copied)	مقلد	*muqal-lad*
immediate	فوري	*fawreyy*
imperfect	معيب	*ma'eeb*
important	مهم	*muhimm*
imported (adj)	مستورد	*mustawrad*
impossible	مستحيل	*mustaHeel*
imposter	دجال	*daj-jaal, daj-jaaleen*
improve	يحسن	*yuHas-sin*
in	في	*fee*
incense (aromatic)	بخور	*bukhoor*
inch	بوصة	*booSa, booSaat*
include	يشمل	*yashmal*
incorrect	غير صحيح	*ghair saHeeH*
increase (v)	يزيد	*yazeed*
indecent	فاضح	*faaDiH*
independent	مستقل	*musta-qill*
indigestion	عسر هضم	*'usr haDm*
inevitable	محتوم	*maHtoom*
inexpensive	رخيص	*rakheeS*
infant	طفل	*Tifl, aTfaal*
infectious	معد	*mu'di*
inflammable	سريع الاشتعال	*saree' l-ishti'aal*
inflammation (n)	ورم	*waram, awraam*
inform	يبلـ–	*yubal-ligh*
information	معلومات	*ma'loomaat*
ingredients	مكونات	*mukaw-winaat*
inject (v)	يحقن	*yaHqin*
injury	إصابة	*iSaaba, iSaabaat*
innocent (not guilty)	بريء	*baree'*
inoculation	تطعيم	*taT'eem*
insect	حشرة	*Hashra, Hashraat*
inside	داخل	*daakhil*
insist	يصر	*yuSirr*

insomnia	أرق	*araq*
instead of	بدلا عن	*badalan 'an*
instrument	آلة	*aala, aalaat*
insult (n)	إهانة	*ihaana, ihaanaat*
insurance	تأمين	*ta'meen*
intend (v)	ينوي	*yanwee*
interior (adj)	داخلي	*daakhileyy*
international	دولي	*duwaleyy*
interpreter	مترجم	*mutarjim*
intestinal	معوي	*ma'aweyy*
intoxicated (adj)	سكران	*sakraan, sakaara*
intruder	دخيل	*dakheel, dukhalaa'*
invite (v)	يدعو	*yad'oo*
Iraq	العراق	*al-'iraaq*
Iraqi	عراقي	*'iraaqeyy, iraaqey-yeen*
Iran	إيران	*eeraan*
Iranian	إيراني	*eeraaneyy, eeraaney-yeen*
iron (n, metal)	حديد	*Hadeed*
iron (v, press)	يكوي	*yakwee*
Islamic	إسلامي	*islaameyy*
island	جزيرة	*jazeera, juzur*
itching	حكة	*Hak-ka*
ivory	عاج	*'aaj*

J

jab (n, injection)	حقنة	*Huqna*
jail (n)	سجن	*sijn*
jam (n)	مربى	*murab-baa*
jasmine	ياسمين	*yasmeen*
jaw	فك	*fakk*
jellyfish	قنديل البحر	*qandeel al-baHr*
Jerusalem	القدس	*al-quds*
Jew(ish)	يهودي	*yahoodeyy, yahood*
jeweler	جوهرجي	*jawharjeyy*
job	وظيفة	*waDHeefa, waDHaa'if*
join (v, connect)	يضم	*yaDumm*

join (v, enroll)	ينضم	yanDamm
Jordan	الأردن	al-urdunn
Jordanian	أردني	urdunneyy, urdunney-yeen
journalist	صحافي	SaHaafeyy, SaHafey-yeen
journey	رحلة	riHla, riHlaat
joy	سرور	suroor
jump (v)	يقفز	yaqfiz
junk	خردة	khurda
just (adj, fair)	عادل	'aadil
just (adv, only)	فقط	faqat
justice (n)	عدالة	'adaala
juvenile (adj)	صبياني	Sibyaaneyy

K

Kaaba (in Mecca)	الكعبة	al-kaa'ba
Kabyle (in Algeria)	القبائل	al-kabaa'il
karate	كاراتيه	karataih
kebob	كباب	kabaab
keep (v, retain)	يحتفظ	yaHtafiDH
keeper (n, of park, etc.)	حارس	Haaris, Hur-raas
kennel (n, dog)	بيت الكلب	bayt al-kalb, buyoot al-kilaab
kerosene	الكيروسين	keeroseen
ketchup	كتشب	kitshab
kettle	غلاية الماء	ghallaayat al-maa'
key	مفتاح	muftaaH, mafaateeH
keyboard (computer, etc.)	لوحة مفاتيح	lawHat mafaateeH
keyhole	ثقب المفتاح	thuqb al-moftaaH
khaki (n, color)	كاكي	kaakee
khamsin winds	رياح الخماسين	riyaaH al-khamaaseen
khedive	الخديوي	al-khudaywee
kid (child)	طفل	Tifl, aTfaal
kidnap (n)	اختطاف	ikhtiTaaf
kidney	كلية	kilya
kidney beans	لوبياء	loobyaa

kill (v)	يقتل	yaqtil
kilogram	كيلوجرام	keelograam
kilometer	كيلومتر	keelomitr
kin (next of)	أقرب الأقرباء	aqrab al-aqribaa'
kind (n, type)	نوع	naw'
kind (adj, good-natured)	طيب	Tay-yib
kindergarten	روضة أطفال	rawDat aTfaal
king	ملك	malik, muluuk
kingdom	مملكة	mamlaka, mamaalik
kiosk	كشك	kushk, akshaak
Kirman (carpets, etc.)	الكرمانية	al-kirmaney-ya
kiss (n)	قبلة	qubla, qublaat
kitchen	مطبخ	maTbakh, maTaabikh
kleptomania	داء السرقة	daa' as-sirqa
knee	ركبة	rukba, rukab
kneepad	وقاء الركبة	wiqaa' ar-rukba
kneel	يركع	yarka'
knick-knacks	خردوات	khurdawaat
knife (n)	سكين	sik-keen, sakaakeen
knob (n, handle, etc.)	مقبض	miqbaD, maqaabiD
knob (n, of butter, etc.)	كبشة	kabsha, kabshaat
knock (v, on door, etc.)	يطرق	yaTruq
knot	عقدة	'uqda
know	يعلم	ya'lam
know-how	مهارة	mahaara
kohl	كحل	koHl
Koran	القرآن الكريم	al-quraan al-kareem
kosher	مباح لليهود	mubaaH lil-yahood
Kurd	كردي	kurdeyy, akraad
Kuwait	الكويت	al-kuwait
Kuwaiti	كويتي	kuwaiteyy, kuwaitey-yeen

L

laboratory	معمل	ma'mal, ma'aamil
labor pains	آلام الوضع	aalaam al-waD'
Labor Party	حزب العمال	Hizb al-'ummaal

Labor Day	عيد العمال	'eed al-'ummaal
lace (n)	دنتلة	dantella
ladder	سلم	sil-lim, salaalim
ladle	مغرفة	maghrafa, maghaarif
lady	سيدة	sayyeda, sayyedaat
lake	بحيرة	buHaira, buHairaat
lamb (young sheep)	حمل	Hamal
lamb (meat)	ضاني صغير	Daanee Sagheer
lamp	مصباح	miSbaaH, maSaabeeH
land (n)	أرض	arD, araaDi
land (v)	يهبط	yahbiT
landmarks	معالم	ma'aalim
landscape (n, view)	منظر	manDHar, manaaDHir
landscape (adj. horizontal)	أفقي	ufuqeyy
language	لغة	lugha, lughaat
lantern	فانوس	fanoos, fawaanees
large	كبير	kabeer
laryngitis	التهاب الحنجرة	iltihaab al-hanjara
last (adj, final)	أخير	akheer
lasting	باق	baaqi
late	متأخر	muta'akh-khir
lather	رغوة	raghwa
lattice window	مشربية	mashrabeyya, mashrabey-yaat
laugh (v)	يضحك	yaD-Hak
laughter	ضحك	DaHik
launch (n, motorboat)	زورق سريع	zawraq saree'
launch (v, new product, etc.)	يطلق	yuTliq
laundry (n, clothes)	غسيل	ghaseel
laundry (n, facility)	مغسلة	maghsala
lavender (n, plant)	اللاوندة	al-lawanda
lavender (n, color)	بنفسجي فاتح	banafsajeyy faatiH
law	القانون	al-qaanoon, al-qawaaneen
lawyer	محام	muHaami, muHaami-yeen
laxative	ملين	mulay-yin, mulay-yinaat

layer (n)	طبقة	Tabaqa, Tabaqaat
lazy	كسول	kasool, kasaala
lead (n, metal)	رصاص	ruSaaS
leader (n, chief)	قائد	qaa'id, qaada
leaf	ورقة شجر	waraqat shajar, awraaq shajar
leak (n)	تنقيط	tanqeeT
lean (adj, meat)	خالي الدهن	khaali ad-dihin
leap (n)	قفزة	qafza, qafzaat
learn (v)	يتعلم	yata'allam
lease (v)	يؤجر	yu'aj-jir
least (adj)	أقل	aqall
leather	جلد	jild
leave (v, abandon)	يترك	yatruk
leave (n, vacation)	عطلة	'uTla, 'uTlaat
Lebanese	لبناني	lubnaaneyy, lubnacney-yeen
Lebanon	لبنان	lubnaan
lecture (n)	محاضرة	muHaadara, muHaadaraat
left (opp. right)	يسار	yasaar
left-handed	أشول	ashwal
leg	رجل	rijl, arjul
legal	قانوني	qanooneyy
legend (myth)	أسطورة	usToora, asaaTeer
lemon	ليمون أصفر	laymoon aSfar
lemonade	ليمونادة	laymoonada
lend	يعير	yu'eer
length	طول	Tool
lens	عدسة	adasa, adasaat
Lent	صيام المسيحيين	Siyaam al-maseeHey-yeen
lentils	عدس	'ads
less (adj, fewer)	أقل	aqall
lesson	درس	dars, duroos
let (rent out)	يؤجر	yu'aj-jir
let (allow)	يسمح	yasmaH
lethal	مميت	mumeet
lethargy	خمول	khumool
letter (mail)	خطاب	khiTaab

letter (alphabet)	حرف	*Harf, Huroof*
lettuce	خس	*khass*
Levant	المشرق العربي	*al-mashriq al-'arabi*
level (n, height reached)	مستوى	*mustawa, mustawayaat*
library	مكتبة	*maktaba, maktabaat*
Libya	ليبيا	*leebya*
Libyan	ليبي	*leebeyy, leebey-yeen*
license	ترخيص	*tarkheeS, taraakheeS*
life	حياة	*Hayaa*
lifeboat	قارب النجاة	*qaarib an-najaah, qawaarib an-najaah*
lifebuoy	طوق النجاة	*Tawq an-najaah, aTwaaq an-najaah*
light (adj, opp. heavy)	خفيف	*khafeef*
light (n, sunlight, etc.)	ضوء	*Daw', aDwaa'*
lighthouse	فنارة	*fanaara*
lightning	برق	*barq*
like (similar to)	مثل	*mithl*
like (v, enjoy)	يحب أن	*yuHibb ann*
limbs	أطراف	*aTraaf*
lime (citrus fruit)	ليمون أخضر	*laymoon akhDar*
limit	حد	*Hadd, Hudood*
limp (v)	يعرج	*ya'ruj*
line	خط	*khaTT, khuTooT*
linen	بياضات	*bayaDaat*
link	وصلة	*waSla, waSlaat*
lip	شفاه	*shifaah*
lipstick	أحمر شفاة	*aHmar shifaah*
liquid	سائل	*saa'il, sawaa'il*
liquor	مشروبات روحية	*mashroobaat rawHey-ya*
list (n)	قائمة	*qaa'ima, qawaa'im*
listen	يستمع	*yastami'*
literature	أدب	*adab*
liter	لتر	*litr*
litigation	إجراءات قضائية	*ijraa'aat qaDaa'ey-ya*
litter	زبالة	*zibaala*

little	صغير	Sagheer
live (v, dwell)	يسكن	yaskun
live (adj, wire, etc.)	حي	Hayy
lively	نابض	naabiD
liver	كبد	kabid
lizard	سحلية	siHliyya, saHaali
load (n, cargo, etc.)	حمل	Himl, aHmaal
loaf (n, bread)	رغيف	ragheef, arghifa
loan (n)	قرض	qarD, qurooD
local	محلي	maHal-leyy
lock (n, fastening)	قفل	qifl, aqfaal
lock (v)	يقفل	yaqfil
locksmith	صانع أقفال	Saani' aqfaal
lodging	مكان إقامة	makaan iqaama
logic	منطق	manTiq
lonely	وحيد	waHeed
long (adj, lengthy)	طويل	Taweel
long (v, miss)	يحن	yaHinn
loofah	لوفة	loofa
look (v, see)	ينظر	yanzhur
look (n, appearance)	مظهر	maDHar, maDHaahir
look out!	احترس!	iHtaris!
loose (adj, free)	طليق	Taleeq
loose (adj, baggy)	واسع	waasi'
lorry	شاحنة	shaaHina, shaaHinaat
lose	يفقد	yafqid
loss	خسارة	khusaara
lotus	لوتس	lootos
loud	عالي الصوت	'aali aS-Sawt
lounge (n)	قاعة جلوس	qaa'at jiloos, qaa'aat jiloos
love (n)	حب	Hubb
love (v)	يحب	yuHibb
low	منخفض	munkhafiD
loyal	وفي	wafeyy
lozenge pastille	بستيلية	basteelya
lubrication	تزييت	tazyeet
luck	حظ	HaDH

lucky	محظوظ	maH-DHooDH
luggage	أمتعة	amti'a
lump	ورم	waram, awraam
lunar	قمري	qamareyy
lunch	الغداء	al-ghadaa'
lung	رئة	ri'a
luxurious	فخم	fakhm

M

macaroni	مكرونة	makarona
mad (angry)	غضبان	ghaDbaan, ghaDbaaneen
mad (crazy)	مجنون	majnoon, majaaneen
magazine (periodical)	مجلة	majal-la, majal-laat
magistrate	قاض أول	qaaDi aw-wal
magnesium milk	محلول المجنيزيا	maHlool al-magneezya
maid	خادمة	khadima, khadimaat
mail (n, letters)	بريد	bareed
mail (v)	يرسل بالبريد	yursil bil-bareed
main (adj, central)	رئيسي	ra'eeseyy
maintenance (servicing)	صيانة	Siyaana
maize	ذرة	Dhur-ra
major (at university)	التخصص الدراسي	at-takhaS-SuS ad-diraaseyy
majority	أغلبية	aghlabey-ya
make (n, brand, etc.)	طراز	Tiraaz, Tiraazaat
make (v, manufacture, etc.)	يصنع	yaSna'
make-up (n, lipstick, etc.)	مكياج	mikyaaj
malaria	ملاريا	malarya
male	ذكر	dhakar, dhukoor
mallet	مطرقة خشبية	miTraqa khashabey-ya
malt	شعير	sha'eer
man	رجل	rajul, rijaal

management (n)	إدارة	idaara
mandatory	إجباري	ijbaareyy
mango	مانجو	mango
manicure	تجميل أظافر اليد	tajmeel aDHaafir al-yad
mansion	بيت فخم	bait fakhm, buyoot fakhma
manual (adj, by hand)	يدوي	yadaweyy
manual (n, booklet)	دليل مطبوع	daleel maTboo'
manufacture (v)	يصنع	yaSna'
many	كثير	katheer
map	خريطة	khareeTa, kharaa'iT
marble (n, stone)	رخام	rukhaam
March	مارس	maaris
mare	فرسة	farasa, farasaat
margarine	مرجرين	marjareen
marinade (v)	يتبل	yutab-bil
marine (adj)	بحري	baHreyy
market (n)	سوق	sooq, aswaaq
market (v)	يسوق	yusaw-wiq
marketing	تسويق	tasweeq
marmalade	مربى البرتقال	murabba al-burtuqaal
Maronite	ماروني	maarooneyy, marooney-yeen
marriage	زواج	zawaaj
marrow	نخاع	nukhaa'
marry	يتزوج	yatazaw-waj
marvelous	مذهل	mudh-hil
mascara	مسكارا	maskaara
masculine	مذكر	mudhakkar
mash (v)	يهرس	yahris
mask (n)	قناع	qinaa', aqni'a
mass (church service)	قداس	qud-daas
massage	تدليك	tadleek
massive	ضخم	Dakhm
masterpiece	تحفة	tuHfa, tuHaf
mat	سجادة صغيرة	sij-jaada Sagheera
match (n, sport)	مباراة	mubaaraah
match-box	علبة كبريت	ulbat kibreet
matches	كبريت	kibreet

material (n, fabric)	قماش	qumaash, aqmisha
mathematics	رياضيات	riyaaDiyaat
matinee	حفلة بالنهار	Hafla bin-nahaar
mattress	مرتبة	martaba, maraatib
mausoleum	ضريح	DareeH, aDreHa
maximum	أقصى	aqSaa
maybe	ربما	rub-bama
mayor	عمدة	'umda, 'umad
me	أنا	ana
meal	وجبة	wajba, wajbaat
meaning	معنى	ma'naa
measles	حصبة	HaSba
measurement	قياس	qiyaas
meat	لحم	laHm
Mecca	مكة	makka
mechanic	ميكانيكي	mekaneeki
medical	طبي	Tib-beyy
medicine	دواء	dawaa'
medium (adj)	متوسط	mutawas-siT
meet (v)	يلتقي	yaltaqee
melon	شمام	sham-maam
melt	يذوب	yadhoob
membership (n)	عضوية	'uDwey-ya
memento	تذكار	tidhkaar
memories	ذكريات	dhikrayaat
mend	يصلح	yuSliH
menu	قائمة	qaa'ima
mess (n, chaos)	فوضى	fawDa
message	رسالة	risaala
metal	معدن	ma'dan
middle	وسط	waSaT
midnight	منتصف الليل	muntaSaf al-lail
migraine	صداع نصفي	Sudaa' niSfeyy
mild	خفيف	khafeef
military (adj)	عسكري	'askaree
milk	حليب	Haleeb
minaret	مئذنة	mi'dhana, ma'aadhin

mine	لي	lee
mineral water	مياه معدنية	miyaah ma'daney-ya
minimum charge	حد أدنى	Hadd adnaa
mint (n, herb)	نعناع	ni'naa'
minute (n, time)	دقيقة	daqeeqa, daqaa'iq
mirage	سراب	saraab
mirror	مرآة	mir'aah, miraayaat
miserable (sad)	تعيس	ta'ees
misfortune (bad luck)	نحس	naHs
missing (adj, not found)	مفقود	mafqood, mafqoodeen
mistake (n)	غلطة	ghalTa, ghalaTaat
misunderstanding	سوء فهم	soo' fahm
mixture	خليط	khaleeT
mobile	متنقل	mutanaq-qil
moderate (adj)	معتدل	mu'tadil
modern	عصري	'aSree
moment	لحظة	laHdha, laHdhaat
monastery	دير	dair, adyira
money	مال	maal
month	شهر	shahr, shuhoor
monthly	شهري	shahreyy
monuments	آثار	aathaar
moon	قمر	qamar, aqmaar
more	أكثر	akthar
morning	صباح	SabaaH
Moroccan	مغربي	maghribeyy, maghaariba
Morocco	المغرب	al-maghrib
mosque	مسجد	masjid, masaajid
mosquito	باعوضة	baa'ooDa, baa'ooD
mother (n)	أم	umm
mountain	جبل	jabal, jibaal
mouth	فم	fam
move (v)	يتحرك	yataHar-rak
movie	فيلم	film, aflaam
muezzin	مؤذن	mu'adh-dhin, mu'adh-dhineen
mufti	مفتي	mufti

mummy	موميا،	mumya'a, mumyawaat
muscle	عضلة	'aDala, 'aDalaat
museum	متحف	matHaf, mataaHif
music	موسيقى	museeqa
mystery	سر	sirr, asraar
myth	خرافة	khuraafa, khurafaat

N

name	اسم	ism, asmaa'
narrow	ضيق	Day-yiq
nationality	جنسية	jinsey-ya, jinsey-yaat
natural	طبيعي	Tabi'eyy
near	قريب	qareeb
necessary	ضروري	Darooreyy
neck	رقبة	raqba
need (n)	حاجة	Haaja, Haajaat
need (v)	يحتاج	yaHtaaj
nephew (son of brother)	ابن أخ	ibn akh
nephew (son of sister)	ابن أخت	ibn ukht
nerve	عصب	'aSab, a'Saab
never	أبدا	abadan
new	جديد	jadeed
news	خبر	khabar, akhbaar
newspaper	جريدة	jareeda, jaraa'id
newsstand	كشك الجرائد	kushk al-jaraa'id
next	تال	taali
niece (daughter of brother)	بنت أخ	bint akh
niece (daughter of sister)	بنت أخت	bint ukht
night	ليل	lail, layaali
Nile	النيل	an-neel
nobody	لا أحد	laa aHad
noise	ضجيج	Dajeej
nomad	رحال	raH'Haal
normal	عادي	'aadeyy

north	شمال	shamaal
nose	أنف	anf
nothing	لا شئ	laa shai'
now	الآن	al-aan
Nubia	النوبة	an-nooba
Nubian	نوبي	noobeyy, noobey-yeen
nuisance (adj)	مزعج	muz'ij
number	رقم	raqm, arqaam
nurse	ممرضة	mumar-riDa, momar-riDaat
nuts (adj, crazy)	مخبول	makhbool
nuts (n, walnuts, etc.)	مكسرات	mukas-saraat

O

oasis	واحة	waaHa, waaHaat
obelisk	مسلة	misal-la, misal-laat
obligatory	اجباري	ijbaareyy
obtain	يحصل على	yaHSul 'alaa
obvious	واضح	waaDiH
occasion	مناسبة	munaasaba, munaasabaat
ocean	محيط	muHeeT, muHeeTaat
offence (n, crime)	جريمة	jareema, jaraa'im
offence (n, insult)	إساءة	isaa'a, isaa'aat
offer (n)	عرض	'arD, 'urooD
offer (v)	يعرض	ya'raD
office	مكتب	maktab, makaatib
officer (military)	ضابط	DaabiT, Dub-baaT
oil	زيت	zait, zuyoot
okra	بامية	bamya
old (object)	قديم	qadeem
old (person)	مسن	musinn
olive	زيتونة	zaitoona, zaitoon
Oman	عمان	'umaan
Omani	عماني	'umaaneyy, umaaney-yeen
on	على	'ala
once	مرة	mar-ra
onion	بصل	baSal

only	فقط	faqaT
open (adj)	مفتوح	maftooH
operation	عملية	'amaley-ya, 'amaley-yaat
opportunity	فرصة	furSa, furaS
opposite	عكس	'aks
optician	نظاراتي	naDH-DHaraati
optional	اختياري	ikhti-yaareyy
or	أو	aw
orange (adj, color)	برتقالي	burtuqaaleyy
orange (n, fruit)	برتقال	burtuqaala, burtuqaal
order (n, method)	نظام	niDHaam
order (v, demand)	يأمر	ya'mur
ordinary	عادي	'aadeyy
organic	عضوي	'uDwee
organize (v)	ينظم	yunaDH-DHim
oriental	شرقي	sharqeyy
orientalist	مستشرق	mustashriq, mustashriqeen
original (adv)	أصلي	aSleyy
ornamental	زخرفي	zukhrufi
other	آخر	aakhar
ours	لنا	lina
outside	في الخارج	fil-khaarij
oven	فرن	furn
overland	برا	bar-ran
oversight	سهو	sahw
owe	يدين	yadeen
owner	مالك	maalik

P

pack (v)	يحزم	yaHzim
package (n)	طرد	Tard, Turood
package (v)	يغلف	yughal-lif
padlock (n)	قفل	qifl, aqfaal
pain (n)	ألم	alam
palace	قصر	qaSr, quSoor
pale (adj)	شاحب	shaaHib

Palestine	فلسطين	falasTeen
Palestinian	فلسطيني	falasTeeneyy, falasTeeney-yeen
palm (n, anatomical)	كف	kaff
palm tree	نخلة	nakhla, nakhl
pamphlet	كتيب	kutay-yib
panic (n)	هلع	hala'
paper (n, sheet, etc.)	ورق	waraq, awraaq
papyrus	ورق البردي	waraq al-bardi
paradise	فردوس	firdaws
parasite	طفيلي	Tofaileyy
pardon (n, amnesty)	عفو	'afw
parents	أبوين	abawain
park (n, gardens)	حديقة	Hadeeqa, Hadaa'iq
park (v, cars, etc.)	يصف	yaSuff
part (n, section)	جزء	juz', ajzaa'
partner (n)	شريك	shareek, shurakaa'
party (n, ball)	حفلة	Hafla, Haflaat
party (n, political)	حزب	Hizb, aHzaab
pass (n, permit)	تصريح	taSreeH, taSaareeH
pass (v, go past)	يمر	yamurr
passenger	راكب	raakib, ruk-kaab
passport	جواز سفر	jawaaz safar
past (adj)	ماض	maaDi
paternal	أبوي	abaweyy
path	ممر	mamarr
patience (n)	صبر	Sabr
patient (n, sick person)	مريض	mareeD, marDaa
pay (v)	يدفع	yadfa'
peace	سلام	salaam
pearl	لؤلؤة	lu'lu'a, lu'lu'
peas	بازلاء	bazilaa'
pencil	قلم رصاص	qalam ruSaaS
people	ناس	naas
pepper (n)	فلفل	filfil
perfect	كامل	kaamil
performance	عرض	'arD, urooD

permit (v)	يسمح	yasmaH
person	شخص	shakhS, ash-khaaS
Pharaonic	فرعوني	fir'awneyy
pharmacy	صيدلية	Saydaley-ya, Saydaley-yaat
phonecard	كارت التليفون	kart at-tilifon
photographer	مصور	muSaw-wir, muSaw-wireen
pick (v, choose)	يختار	yakhtaar
picture (n, photo, etc.)	صورة	Soora, Suwar
piece (n)	قطعة	qiT'a, qiTa'
pierce	يثقب	yathqub
pilgrim	حاج	Haajj, Hujjaaj
pilgrimage (to Mecca)	الحج	al-Hajj
pill	قرص	qurS, aqraaS
pin (n)	دبوس	dab-boos, dabaabees
place (n, location)	مكان	makaan, amaakin
plant (n)	نبات	nabaat, nabaataat
plant (v)	يزرع	yazra'
plate (n, dish)	صحن	saHn, SuHoon
platform (n, for train)	رصيف	raSeef, arSifa
play (n)	مسرحية	masraHey-ya, masraHey-yaat
play (v)	يلعب	yal'ab
plenty	كثير	katheer
plug (n)	سدادة	sad-daada
plumber	سباك	sab-baak
pocket (n)	جيب	jaib, juyoob
point (n, dot)	نقطة	nuqTa, nuqaTT
point (v)	يشير	yusheer
polite	مؤدب	mu'ad-dab
pomegranate	رمان	rum-maan
pool (n, pond, etc.)	بركة	birka, birak
popular	شعبي	sha'bee
port	ميناء	meena', mawaani'
porter	حمال	Ham-maal, Ham-maaleen
positive	ايجابي	eejaabee
possibility	احتمال	iHtimaal
post office	مكتب البريد	maktab al-bareed

postcard	بطاقة بريدية	biTaqa bareedey-ya
pottery	فخار	fukh-khaar
powder	مسحوق	masHooq, masaaHeeq
prawns (shrimp)	جمبري	jambaree (coll.)
pray (v)	يصلي	yuSal-lee
precious	نفيس	nafees
precisely	بدقة	bi-diq-qa
prefer	يفضل	yufaD-Dil
pregnant	حامل	Haamil
prescription	روشتة	rooshet-ta
press (n, media)	صحافة	SaHaafa
press (n, printing)	مطبعة	maTba'a, maTaabi'
press (v, iron)	يكوي	yakwee
press (v, push)	يدفع	yadfa'
pretty	جميل	jameel
prey	فريسة	fareesa
price (n)	سعر	si'r, as'aar
prince	أمير	ameer, umaraa'
princess	أميرة	ameera, ameeraat
prison	سجن	sijn, sujoon
private	خاص	khaaS
problem	مشكلة	mushkila, mashaakil
professional	محترف	muHtarif, muHtarifeen
prohibited	ممنوع	mamnoo'
promise (n)	وعد	wa'd, wu'ood
proof	برهان	burhaan
prophet	رسول	rasool
province	إقليم	iqleem, aqaaleem
provincial	ريفي	reefeyy
pull (v)	يسحب	yasHab
puncture (n)	ثقب	thuqb, thuqoob
pure	نقي	naqeyy
purple	بنفسجي	banafsajeyy
push (v)	يدفع	yadfa'
put	يضع	yadaa'
pyramid	هرم	haram, ahraam

Q

Qatar	قطر	qaTar
Qatari	قطري	qaTareyy, qaTarey-yeen
quaint	طريف	Tareef
quality (n)	جودة	jawda
quantity (n)	كمية	kim-mey-ya
quarrel (v)	يتشاجر	yatashaajar
quarter (n)	ربع	rub'
queen	ملكة	malika, malikaat
question (n)	سؤال	su'aal, as'ila
quick	سريع	saree'
quiet (adj)	هادئ	haadi'
quit	يهجر	yahjur

R

rabbi	حاخام	Haakhaam
rabbit	أرنب	arnab, araanib
race (n, running, etc.)	سباق	sibaaq, sibaaqaat
railroad	سكة حديد	sikka Hadeed
rain (n)	مطر	maTar
raise (v)	يرفع	yarfa'
raisin	زبيب	zibeeb
Ramadan	رمضان	ramaDaan
rare (uncommon)	نادر	naadir
rash (n)	طفح جلدي	TafH jildee
rat	جرذ	jurdh, jurdhaan
rate (n)	معدل	mu'ad-dal
raw	نيء	nayy'
razor	موس حلاقة	moos Hilaaqa
reach (v)	يصل	yaSil
read	يقرأ	yaqra'
ready (adj)	جاهز	jaahiz
real	حقيقي	Haqeeqeyy
reason (n, cause)	سبب	sabab, asbaab
reasonable	معقول	ma'qool

rebate	خصم	khaSm
receipt	إيصال	eeSaal, eeSaalaat
receive	يستلم	yastalim
reception (n, hotel)	استقبال	istiqbaal
recipe	وصفة	waSfa, waSfaat
recommendation	توصية	tawSey-ya
recover (from illness)	يشفى	yushfa
rectangle	مستطيل	mustaTeel, mustaTeelaat
reduce	يقلل	yuqal-lil
reef	صخور بحرية	Sukhoor baHrey-ya
refill (v)	يملأ	yamla'
refresh	ينعش	yun'ish
refreshments	مرطبات	muraT-Tibaat
refuse (v)	يرفض	yarfuD
regional	إقليمي	iqleemee
regret (v)	يأسف	ya'saf
relationship	علاقة	'ilaaqa, 'ilaaqaat
relative (n)	قريب	qareeb, aqaarib
relax	يستجم	yastajim
reliable	موثوق به	mawthooq bih
relic	أثر	athar, aathaar
religion	دين	deen, adyaan
remain	يبقى	yabqa
remedy (n)	علاج	'ilaaj
remember	يتذكر	yatadhak-kar
remove	يبعد	yub'id
rent (v)	يؤجر	yu'aj-jir
repair (n)	تصليح	taSleeH
repeat (v)	يكرر	yukar-rir
repellent (n)	طارد	Taarid
reply (n)	رد	radd, rudood
reply (v)	يرد	yarudd
reporter	صحفي	SaHafee, SaHafeeyeen
representative (n)	مندوب	mandoob, mandoobeen
request (n)	طلب	Talab, Talabaat
request (v)	يطلب	yaTlub
rescue (n)	إنقاذ	inqaadh

reservation (n)	حجز	Hajz, Hujuzaat
residential	سكني	sakaneyy
resignation	استقالة	istiqaala
resolve (problem)	يحل (مشكلة)	yaHill (mushkila)
resort (n)	منتجع	muntaja', muntaja'aat
respect (n)	احترام	iHtiraam
respiratory	تنفسي	tanaf-fuseyy
responsible	مسؤول	mas'ool
rest (v)	يستريح	yastareeH
restaurant	مطعم	maT'am, maTaa'im
restoration	تجديد	tajdeed
result (n)	نتيجة	nateeja, nataa'ij
retirement (from work)	تقاعد	taqaa'ud
return (n)	عودة	'awda
return (v)	يعود	ya'ood
reverse (n)	عكس	'aks
reward (n)	مكافأة	mukaafa'a, mukaafa'aat
rice	رز	ruzz
riding (n)	ركوب الخيل	rukoob al-khail
right (opp. left)	يمين	yameen
right (correct)	صحيح	saHeeH
right (n, entitlement)	حق	Haqq, Huqooq
rise (v)	يرتفع	yartafi'
risk (n)	مجازفة	mujaazafa, mujaazafaat
road	طريق	Tareeq, Turuq
rock	صخرة	Sakhra, Sokhoor
roof	سقف	saqf, suqoof
room (n, hotel, etc.)	حجرة	Hujra, Hujraat
root (n)	جذر	jidhr, judhoor
rope	حبل	Habl, Hibaal
rosary	سبحة	sibHa
rose	زهرة	zahra, zuhoor
Rosetta	رشيد	rasheed
rough (adj, not smooth)	خشن	khashin
round (adj, spherical)	مستدير	mustadeer
round-trip	ذهاب وعودة	dhihaab wa 'awda
route (n)	خط سير	khaTT sair

rubber ring	عوامة	'aw-waama
ruby (n)	ياقوت	yaaqoot
rug	سجادة	sij-jaada, sajaajeed
ruins	أطلال	aTlaal
run (v, jog)	يجري	yajree
run (v, operate)	يدير	yudeer
rural	قروي	qaraweyy
rush (v)	يسرع	yusri'
rustic	ريفي	reefeyy
rye (n)	شيلم	shailam

S

sacred (adj)	مقدس	muqad-das
sad	حزين	Hazeen
saddle (n)	سرج	sarj
safe (adj, opp. risky)	مأمون	ma'moon
safe (n, secure box)	خزنة	khazna, khizan
saffron	زعفران	za'faraan
sail (n)	شراع	shiraa'
sailor	بحار	baH-Haar, baH-Haara
saint	قديس	qid-dees, qid-deeseen
sale (n, discount)	أوكازيون	okazyon, okazyonaat
salesman	مندوب مبيعات	mandoob mabee'aat, mandoobeen mabee'aat
salt (n)	ملح	malH, amlaaH
same (adj)	ذاته	dhaatuh
sample (n)	عينة	'ay-yina, 'ay-yinaat
sample (v)	يجرب	yujar-rib
sand (n)	رمل	raml, rimaal
sanitary	صحي	SiH-Heyy
sarcophagus	تابوت حجري	taaboot Hajareyy
satellite	قمر صناعي	qamar Sinaa'eyy
satisfaction	رضا	riDaa
saucepan	كسرولة	kasarol-la
Saudi (Arabia)	السعودية	as-sa'oodey-ya
Saudi (Arabian)	سعودي	sa'oodeyy, sa'oodey-yeen

sausages	سجق	sujuq
save (v, rescue)	ينقذ	yunqidh
save (v, set aside)	يدخر	yad-dakhir
say (v)	يقول	yaqool
scalp (n)	فروة الرأس	farwat ar-ra's
scenery	منظر	manDHar, manaaDHir
school (n)	مدرسة	madrasa, madaaris
screen (n)	ستار	sitaar
scuba diving (n)	غطس	ghaTs
sea	بحر	baHr
search (v)	يبحث	yabHath
season (n, spring, etc.)	فصل	faSl, fuSool
season (v, add spices)	يتبل	yutab-bil
seat (n)	كرسي	kurseyy, karaasee
second (n, after first)	ثان	thaani
second (n, time)	ثانية	thaanya, thawaani
secret (n)	سر	sirr, asraar
secret (adj)	سري	sir-reyy
security (n)	أمن	amn
sedative	مسكن	musak-kin, musak-kinaat
see	يرى	yara
seizure (n, fit)	نوبة	nawba, nawbaat
select	يختار	yakhtaar
sell	يبيع	yabee'
send	يرسل	yursil
sensitive	حساس	Has-saas
separately	منفصلين	munfaSileen
serious	جدي	jid-deyy
service (n, favor)	خدمة	khidma, khidmaat
set (adj, fixed)	محدد	muHad-dadd
set (n, specific group)	طقم	Taqm, aTqum
set (v, clock, etc.)	يضبط	yaDbuT
set (v, place aside)	يحتجز	yaHtajiz
settle (v, pay)	يسدد	yusad-did
shade (n)	ظل	DHil, DHilaal
shape (n)	شكل	shakl, ashkaal
shares (n)	أسهم	ashum

shark	سمكة القرش	samakat al-qirsh
shave (v)	يحلق	yaHlaq
sheet	ملاءة	milaa'a, milaa'aat
sheik	شيخ	shaikh, shuyookh
ship (n)	سفينة	safeena, sufun
shipment (n)	شحنة	shuHna, shuHnaat
shirt (n)	قميص	qameeS, qumSaan
shock (n)	صدمة	Sadma, Sadmaat
shoe	حذاء	Hidhaa', aHdheya
shoelace	رباط الحذاء	ribaaT al-hizhaa'
shop (n)	محل	maHal, maHal-laat
shop (v)	يتسوق	yatasaw-waq
shopping mall	سوق مول	sooq mol
short (adj, opp. long)	قصير	qaSeer
shoulder (n)	كتف	katif, aktaaf
show (n, spectacle)	عرض	'arD, 'urooD
show (v, display)	يعرض	ya'riD
shower (n)	دش	dush
shrimp	جمبري	gambari (coll.)
shrine	ضريح	DareeH, aDreHa
shut (v)	يقفل	yaqfil
sick	مريض	mareeD
side (n)	ناحية	naaHiya, nawaaHi
sign (n, display board)	لافتة	laafita, laafitaat
sign (n, mark)	علامة	'alaama, 'alaamaat
sign (v, check, etc.)	يوقع	yuwaq-qi'
signature	توقيع	tawqee', tawqee'aat
silence (n)	صمت	Samt
silk (adj)	حريري	Hareereyy
silk (n)	حرير	Hareer
silver (adj)	فضي	faD-Deyy
silver (n)	فضة	faD-Da
similarity	تشابه	tashaabuh
simple	بسيط	baseeT
sing	يغني	yughan-nee
sink (n)	حوض	HawD, aHwaaD
sister	أخت	ukht, akhawaat

sit	يجلس	*yajlis*
size (n)	حجم	*Hajm, aHjaam*
skill (n)	مهارة	*mahaara, mahaaraat*
skimmed (adj, milk)	مقشود	*maqshood*
skin (n)	جلد	*jild*
skirt	جونلة/	*gunel-la, gunel-laat/*
	جيبة	*jeeba, jeebaat*
sky	سماء	*samaa', samawaat*
sleep (v)	ينام	*yanaam*
sleeve (n)	كم	*kumm, akmaam*
slice (n)	شريحة	*shareeHa, sharaa'iH*
slip (v, lose footing)	ينزلق	*yanzaliq*
slippers	شبشب	*shibshib, shabaashib*
slow (adj)	بطيء	*baTee'*
small (adj)	صغير	*Sagheer*
smell (n, scent)	رائحة	*raa'iHa, rawaa'iH*
smell (n, sense)	شم	*shamm*
smell (v)	يشم	*yashimm*
smile (n)	ابتسامة	*ibtisaama, ibtisaamaat*
smoke (n)	دخان	*dokh-khaan*
smoke (v)	يدخن	*yudakh-khin*
smooth (adj)	ناعم	*naa'im*
snorkel (n)	أنبوب التنفس	*unboob at-tanaf-fus*
soap (n)	صابون	*Saaboon*
soccer	كرة القدم	*kurat al-qadam*
soft	طري	*Tareyy*
soldier (n)	جندي	*jundeyy, junood*
solution (n, answer)	حل	*Hall, Hulool*
solution (n, liquid)	محلول	*maHlool*
some	بعض	*baa'D*
son	ابن	*ibn, abnaa'*
song	أغنية	*ughneya, aghaani*
sore	ملتهب	*multahib*
sorry	آسف	*aasif*
sound (n)	صوت	*Sawt, aSwaat*
soup	شوربة	*shorba*
speak	يتكلم	*yatakal-lam*

speed (n)	سرعة	sur'a
spices (n)	توابل	tawaabil
spoon (n)	ملعقة	mil'aqa, malaa'iq
sport (n)	رياضة	riyaaDa
spot (n, stain)	بقعة	buq'a, buqa'
spot (v, see)	يلمح	yalmaH
spring (n, season)	الربيع	ar-rabee'
square (n)	مربع	muraba', murab-ba'aat
stamp (n, postage)	طابع بريد	Taabi' bareed
stand (n, position)	موقف	mawqif, mawaaqif
stand (v, opp. sit)	يقف	yaqif
star (n)	نجم	nijm, nujoom
start (v)	يبدأ	yabda'
station (n)	محطة	maHaT-Ta, maHaT-Taat
station (n, police)	قسم البوليس	qism al-bolees
statue	تمثال	timthaal, tamaatheel
stay (v)	يبقى	yabqa
step (n)	خطوة	khaTwa, khaTwaat
stewardess	مضيفة	maDeefa, maDeefaat
stomach (n)	معدة	ma'ida
stone (n)	حجر	Hajar, aHjaar
stop (v)	يقف	yaqif
store (n)	محل	maHall, maHal-laat
storm (n)	عاصفة	'aaSifa, 'awaaSif
story (n, level)	طابق	Taabiq, Tawaabiq
story (n, tale)	قصة	qiS-Sa, qiSaS
straight (direct)	مباشر	mubaashir
strange (adj)	غريب	ghareeb
strawberry	فراولة	farawla
strength	قوة	quw-wa, quw-waat
stretcher	نقالة	naq-qaala
string (cord)	خيط	khaiT, khuyooT
strong	قوي	qaweyy
student (n)	طالب	Taalib, Talaba
study (v)	يدرس	yadrus
style (n)	طراز	Tiraaz, Tiraazat
subject (n, topic)	موضوع	mawDoo', mawDoo'aat

succeed (v, opp. fail)	ينجح	yanjaH
such	كهذا	ka-haazha
Sudan	السودان	as-soodaan
Sudanese	سوداني	soodaaneyy, soodaaney-yeen
sugar (n)	سكر	suk-kar
suggestion	اقتراح	iqtiraaH, iqtiraaHaat
suit (n, clothing)	بذلة	badhla
suitable	مناسب	munaasib
suite (hotel)	جناح	jinaaH, ajniHa
sultan	سلطان	sulTaan
sum (n, total)	مجموع	majmoo'
summer	صيف	Saif
sun (n)	شمس	shams
sunburn (n)	حروق الشمس	Hurooq ash-shams
sunrise	شروق	shorooq
sunset	غروب	ghoroob
sure	واثق	waathiq
surgery (n, clinic)	عيادة	'iyaada, 'iyaadaat
surgery (n, operation)	جراحة	jiraaHa, jiraaHaat
surprise (n)	مفاجأة	mufaaja'a, mufaaja'aat
swallow (v, ingest)	يبلع	yabla'
sweet (adj)	حلو	Hulw
swim (v)	يسبح	yasbaH
Syria	سوريا	surey-yaa
Syrian	سوري	sureyy, surey-yeen
syringe (n)	حقنة	Huqna, Huqan
system	نظام	niDHaam, anDHima

T

table (n)	مائدة	maa'ida, mawaa'id
tablet	قرص	qurS, aqraaS
tailor (n)	ترزي	tarzi, tarzey-ya
take	يأخذ	ya'khudh
talk (v)	يتكلم	yatakal-lam
tapestry	نسيج مزخرف	naseej muzakhraf
taste (n, sense)	تذوق	tadhaw-wuq

tax (n)	ضريبة	Dareeba, Daraa'ib
tea (n)	شاي	shaay
teach	يعلم	yu'al-lim
teacher	معلم	mu'al-lim, mu'al-limeen
tear (n, drop)	دمعة	dam'a, dumoo'
tear (v, shred)	يمزق	yumaz-ziq
teenager	مراهق	muraahiq, muraahiqeen
tell	يخبر	yukhbir
temperature	درجة الحرارة	darajat al-Haraara
temple	معبد	ma'bad, ma'aabid
temporary	مؤقت	mu'aq-qat
tenant (n)	مستأجر	musta'jir, musta'jireen
tent	خيمة	khaima, khiyaam
terminal (n, airport)	مبنى المطار	mabna al-maTaar
terminal (n, bus)	موقف الأوتوبيس	mawqaf al-otobees
terrace (balcony)	شرفة	shurfa, shurfaat
terrible	فظيع	faDHee'
terrific	رائع	raa'i
test (n)	اختبار	ikhtibaar, ikhtibaaraat
textile	نسيج	naseej
thankful (adj)	شاكر	shaakir
theater (n, plays, etc.)	مسرح	masraH, masaariH
theater (n, surgeries, etc.)	غرفة العمليات	ghurfat al-'amaley-yaat
therapy	علاج	'ilaaj
there	هناك	Hunaak
thick	سميك	sameek
thief (n)	لص	liSS, luSooS
thin	نحيف	naHeef
thing	شيء	shai', ashyaa'
thirsty	عطشان	'atshaan
this	هذا	haadha
thoroughbred	أصيل	aSeel
throat	زور	zawr
through (prep)	خلال	khilaal
throw	يرمي	yarmee
thyme	زعتر	za'tar

ticket (n)	تذكرة	tadhkara, tadhaakir
tie (n, neck)	كرافتة	karavatta
tie (v)	يربط	yarbuT
tight	ضيق	Day-yiq
tights	كولونات	kolonaat
time (n, eras, etc.)	زمن	zaman
time (n, of day)	وقت	waqt
tip (n, gratuity)	إكرامية	ikramey-ya, ikramey-yaat
tire (n)	إطار	iTaar, iTaaraat
tire (v)	يتعب	yat'ab
tired (adj)	تعبان	ta'baan
today	اليوم	al-yawm
together (adj)	معا	ma'an
tomato	طماطم	TamaaTim
tomb	مقبرة	maqbara, maqaabir
tomorrow	غدا	ghadan
tongue	لسان	lisaan, alsina
tonight	الليلة	al-laila
tooth	سنة	sin-na, asnaan
top (n)	أعلى	a'la
total (adj, entire)	تام	taam
total (n)	مجموع	majmoo'
touch (v)	يلمس	yalmis
tour (n)	جولة	jawla, jawlaat
tour (v, visit)	يتجول	yatajaw-wal
tourist (n)	سائح	saa'iH, suyaaH
tow (v)	يجر	yajurr
towards (prep)	نحو	naHwa
towel	منشفة	minshafa, manaashif
tower	برج	burj, abraaj
town	مدينة	madeena, mudun
trader	تاجر	taajir, tuj-jaar
traditional (adj)	تقليدي	taqleedeyy
traffic (n, cars, etc.)	مرور	muroor
train (n)	قطار	qiTaar, qiTaaraa
train (v)	يتدرب	yatadar-rab

transfer (n)	تحويل	taHweel, taHweelaat
translator	مترجم	mutarjim, mutarjimeen
transportation	وسيلة تنقل	waseelat tanaq-qul
trash (n)	زبالة	zibaala
travel (v)	يسافر	yusaafir
traveler's checks	شيكات سياحية	sheekaat seyaaHey-ya
treat (v, behave towards)	يعامل	yu'aamil
treat (n, reward)	مكافأة	mukaafa'a
tree	شجرة	shajara, ashjaar
triangle	مثلث	muthal-lath, muthal-lathaat
tribe	قبيلة	qabeela, qabaa'il
trim (n, hair, etc.)	تشذيب	tash-dheeb
trip (n, voyage)	رحلة	riHla, riHlaaat
trip (v, stumble)	يتعثر	yata'ath-thar
trouble (n)	متاعب	mataa'ib
truck (n)	شاحنة	shaaHina, shaaHinaaat
true	حقيقي	Haqeeqeyy
trust (v)	يثق	yathiq
try (v)	يحاول	yuHaawil
Tunis	تونس	toonis
Tunisian	تونسي	tooniseyy, toonisey-yeen
tunnel (n)	نفق	nafaq, anfaaq
Turkey	تركيا	torkeya
turkey	ديك رومي	deek roomeyy
turn (v, go around)	يلف	yalif
turn (v, transform)	يحول	yuHaw-wil
twin	توأم	taw'am, tawaa'im
type (n)	نوع	naw', anwaa'

U

ulcer	قرحة	qurHa
ultimate (adj)	أخير	akheer
umbrella	مظلة	miDHal-la, miDHal-laat
unable	غير قادر	ghair qaadir
unattended	بلا رقابة	bilaa riqaaba

unbearable	لا يطاق	laa yuTaaq
unbelievable	لا يصدق	laa yuSad-daq
uncertain	غير واثق	ghair waathiq
uncle (maternal)	خال	khaal, khilaan
uncle (paternal)	عم	'amm, 'amaam
uncomfortable	غير مريح	ghair mureeH
uncommon	غير مألوف	ghair ma'loof
unconscious	في إغماءة	fee ighmaa'a
uncover	يكشف	yakshif
undecided	متردد	mutarad-did
under (prep)	تحت	taHt
undergraduate	طالب في الجامعة	Taalib fee l-jaami'a
understand	يفهم	yafham
uneasy	قلق	qaliq
unemployment (n)	بطالة	biTaala
unexpected (adj)	مفاجئ	mufaaji'
unhappy	حزين	Hazeen
unhealthy	غير صحي	ghair SiH-Hi
United Arab Emirates	الإمارات العربية المتحدة	al-imaaraat al-'arabey-ya al-muttaHida
United Nations	الأمم المتحدة	al-umam al-muttaHida
United States	الولايات المتحدة	al-wilaayaat al-muttaHida
university	جامعة	jaami'a, jaami'aat
unknown (adj)	مجهول	majhool
unlucky (adj)	سيء الحظ	say-yi' al-HaDH
unofficial	غير رسمي	ghair rasmeyy
unreal	وهمي	wahmeyy
unreasonable	غير معقول	ghair ma'qool
unstable	متقلب	mutaqal-lib
unsuitable	غير مناسب	ghair munaasib
until (prep)	إلى أن	ila 'an
untrue	كاذب	kaadhib
unusual (adj)	نادر	naadir
up	فوق	fawq
upgrade (n)	ترقية	tarqeya
uprising	انتفاضة	intifaaDa
urban (adj)	مدني	madaneyy

use (n)	فائدة	faa'ida, fawaa'id
use (v)	يستخدم	yastakhdim
useful	مفيد	mufeed

V

vacancy (in hotel)	غرف خالية	ghuraf khaaliya
vacancy (for job)	وظائف خالية	waDHaa'if khaaliya
vacate	يخلي	yukhlee
vacation (n)	عطلة	'uTla, 'uTlaat
vaccination	تطعيم	taT'eem
vague (adj)	غامض	ghaamiD
vain	مغرور	maghroor
valid	صالح	SaaliH
valley	واد	waadi, widyaan
valuable	ثمين	thameen
vanish	يختفي	yakhtafee
veal	بتللو	bitel-lo
vegetable(s)	خضار	khuDaar
vegetarian	نباتي	nabaateyy
vehicle	سيارة	say-yaara, say-yaaraat
veil (n)	حجاب	Hijaab
vein (anatomy)	وريد	wareed, awrida
velvet	قطيفة	qaTeefa
ventilation	تهوية	tahwiya
verbal	شفوي	shafaweyy
vernacular (language)	العامية	al-'aamey-ya
veterinary	بيطري	baiTareyy
view (n, opinion)	رأي	ra'yy, aaraa'
view (n, scenery)	منظر	manDHar, manaaDHir
vigilance	يقظة	yaqDHa
village	قرية	qarya, quraa
vinegar	خل	khall
visa	تأشيرة	ta'sheera, ta'sheeraat
visit (n)	زيارة	ziyaara, ziyaaraat
voice (n)	صوت	Sawt, aSwaat
void (adj, invalidated)	باطل	baaTil

voluntary (n)	تطوعي	*tataw-wu'eyy*
volunteer (n)	متطوع	*mutaTaw-wi',*
		mutaTaw-wi'een
vomit (v)	يتقيأ	*yataqay-ya'*
vulgar	سوقي	*sooqeyy*

W

wage (n, salary)	أجر	*ajr, ujoor*
Wailing Wall	حائط المبكى	*Haa'iT al-mabka*
waist	خصر	*khaSr*
wait (v)	ينتظر	*yantaDHir*
waiter (n)	جرسون	*garsoon*
wake (v)	يستيقظ	*yastaiqiDH*
walk (v)	يمشي	*yamshee*
wall	حائط	*Haa'iT, Hawaa'iT*
wallet	حافظة	*HaafiDHa*
want (v)	يريد	*yureed*
war	حرب	*Harb*
ward (hospital)	عنبر	*'anbar, 'anaabir*
warm (adj)	دافئ:	*daafi'*
warranty	ضمان	*Damaan*
wash (v)	يغسل	*yaghsil*
washing machine	غسالة ملابس	*ghas-saalat malaabis*
watch (n, on wrist)	ساعة يد	*saa'at yad*
watch (v, observe)	يراقب	*yuraaqib*
water (n)	ماء	*maa'*
waterfall	شلال	*shal-laal, shal-laalaat*
wave (n, in sea)	موجة	*mawja, amwaaj*
wave (v, with hand)	يلوح	*yulaw-wiH*
wax (n)	شمع	*sham'*
way (n, method)	طريقة	*Tareeqa, Turuq*
way (n, route)	طريق	*Tareeq, Turuq*
weak	ضعيف	*Da'eef*
wealthy	غني	*ghaneyy*
wear	يلبس	*yalbus*
weather (n)	جو	*jaww*

web	شبكة	shabaka
wedding (n)	زفاف	zifaaf
week	أسبوع	usboo', asaabee'
weekly	أسبوعي	usboo'eyy
weight (n)	وزن	wazn, awzaan
welcome (n)	ترحيب	tarHeeb
well (n, for water)	بئر	bi'r, aabaar
well done!	أحسنت!	aHsant
well done (cooking)	مطهو جيدا	maT-hoo jay-yidan
well-known (adj)	مشهور	mash-hoor
west	غرب	gharb
wet (adj)	مبتل	mubtall
what?	ماذا؟	maadha
wheat	قمح	qamH
wheel	عجلة	ajala, ajalaat
when?	متى؟	matta
where?	أين؟	aina
which?	أي؟	ayy
white	أبيض	abyaD
who?	من؟	man
whole (adj)	كامل	kaamil
wholesale	جملة	jumla
why?	لماذا؟	limaazha
wide	عريض	'areeD
widow	أرملة	armala, araamil
widower	أرمل	armal, araamil
wife	زوجة	zawja, zawjaat
wild (adj, reckless)	طائش	Taa'ish
wild (adj, uncultivated)	بري	bar-reyy
will (auxiliary verb)	سوف	sawfa
win (v)	يربح	yarbaH
wind (n)	ريح	reeH, reeyaaH
windmill	طاحونة	TaaHoona, TawaaHeen
window	شباك	shub-baak, shabaabeek
windscreen	زجاج أمامي	zujaaj amaameyy
wine	نبيذ	nabeedh
wing (n)	جناح	jinaaH, ajniHa

winter	شتاء	shitaa'
wipe (v)	يمسح	yamsaH
wish (n)	أمنية	umniya, umniyaat
with (prep)	مع	ma'
withdraw	يسحب	yasHab
woman	امرأة	imra'a, nisaa'
wood (n, timber)	خشب	khashab, akh-shaab
wool	صوف	Soof, aSwaaf
word	كلمة	kalima, kalimaat
work (n, job)	عمل	'amal
world	عالم	'aalam
worm	دودة	dooda, dood
worse	أسوأ	aswa'
worth (n)	قيمة	qeema
wound (n)	جرح	jarH, jiraaH
wreckage	حطام	HuTaam
write (v)	يكتب	yaktub
wrong (adj)	خاطئ	khaaTi'

X, Y, Z

x-ray	أشعة	ashi'aa
yacht	يخت	yakht, yukhoot
year	سنة	sana, sanawaat
yearly	سنوي	sanaweyy
yeast	خميرة	khameera
Yemen	اليمن	al-yaman
Yemeni	يمني	yamaneyy, yamaney-yeen
yesterday	أمس	ams
yogurt	زبادي	zabaadee
young (adj)	صغير السن	sagheer as-sinn
youth price	سعر الشباب	s'ir ash-shabaab
youth hostel	بيت الشباب	bait ash-shabaab
zebra	حمار وحشي	Himaar waH-sheyy
zero	صفر	Sifr
zest (n, lemon)	قشرة	qishra
zoo	حديقة الحيوان	Hadeeqat al-Hayawaan

ARABIC–ENGLISH DICTIONARY

This *Arabic–English Dictionary* is arranged in the order of the Arabic alphabet – see page 9 for reference. Remember Arabic is read from right to left.

Plurals of common words are given in transliteration after the singular. Verbs are listed under the present tense, third person masculine ("he" form), e.g. **yaktub, yadrus**.

(alif) ١

father (n) *ab*	أب
smile (n) *ibtisaama, ibtisaamaat*	ابتسامة
creativity *ibtikaar*	ابتكار
never; ever (adv) *abadan*	أبدا
son *ibn, abnaa'*	ابن
nephew (son of brother) *ibn akh*	ابن أخ
nephew (son of sister) *ibn ukht*	ابن أخت
daughter *ibna, banaat*	ابنة
paternal *abaweyy*	أبوي
parents *abawain*	أبوين
white *abyaD*	أبيض
monuments *aathaar*	آثار
relic *athar, aathaar*	أثر
couple (n) *ithnain*	اثنين
answer (n) *ijaaba, ijaabaat*	إجابة
obligatory; mandatory *ijbaareyy*	إجباري
charge (fee); wage (salary) *ajr, ujoor*	أجر
litigation *ijraa'aat qaDaa'ey-ya*	إجراءات قضائية
price, fare *ujra*	أجرة
foreigner *ajnabee*	أجنبي
caution (prudence) *iHtiraas*	احتراس
respect (n) *iHtiraam*	احترام

look out! **iHtaris!**	احترس!
celebration **iHtifaal, iHtifaalaat**	احتفال
possibility **iHtimaal**	احتمال
best **aHsan**	أحسن
well done! **aHsant**	أحسنت!
lipstick **aHmar shifaah**	أحمر شفاة
brother **akh, ukhwa**	أخ
sister **ukht, akhawaat**	أخت
test (n) **ikhtibaar, ikhtibaaraat**	اختبار
kidnap (n) **ikhtiTaaf**	اختطاف
choice **ikhtiyaar**	اختيار
optional **ikhti-yaareyy**	اختياري
other; another **aakhar**	آخر
last; ultimate (adj) **akheer**	أخير
administration; management **idaara**	إدارة
literature **adab**	أدب
ear **udhun, aadhaan**	أذن
engagement; appointment **irtibaaT, irtibaaTaat**	ارتباط
concussion **irtijaaj**	ارتجاج
altitude **irtifaa', irtifaa'aat**	ارتفاع
Jordanian **urdunneyy, urdunney-yeen**	أردني
land (n) **arD, araaDi**	أرض
floor (n) **arDey-ya**	أرضية
insomnia **araq**	أرق
widower **armal, araamil**	أرمل
widow **armala, araamil**	أرملة
rabbit **arnab, araanib**	أرنب
blue **azraq**	أزرق
azure **azraq samaaweyy**	أزرق سماوي
offence (n, insult) **isaa'a, isaa'aat**	إساءة
base (n, foundation) **asaas**	أساس
elementary (basic) **asaaseyy**	أساسي
week **usboo', asaabee'**	أسبوع
weekly **usboo'eyy**	أسبوعي
break (n, respite) **istiraaHa**	استراحة
consultant **istishaareyy**	استشاري
resignation **istiqaala**	استقالة

reception (n, hotel) *istiqbaal*	استقبال
family *usra, usarr*	أسرة
dynasty (n) *usra Haakima*	أسرة حاكمة
legend (myth) *usToora, asaaTeer*	أسطورة
ambulance *is'aaf*	إسعاف
sorry *aasif*	آسف
below *asfal*	أسفل
ancestors *aslaaf*	أسلاف
Islamic *islaameyy*	إسلامي
name *ism, asmaa'*	اسم
diarrhea *is≠haal*	إسهال
shares (n) *ashum*	أسهم
worse *aswa'*	أسوأ
black (color) *aswad*	أسود
x-ray *ashi'aa*	أشعة
blonde (adj) *ashqar*	أشقر
left-handed *ashwal*	أشول
injury *iSaaba, iSaabaat*	إصابة
finger *iSba', aSaabi'*	إصبع
artificial *iSTinaa'eyy*	اصطناعي
bald *aSla'*	أصلع
original; genuine; authentic *aSleyy*	أصلي
deaf *aSamm*	أصم
thoroughbred *aSeel*	أصيل
extra *iDaafeyy*	إضافي
tire (n) *iTaar, iTaaraat*	إطار
limbs *aTraaf*	أطراف
ruins (n) *aTlaal*	أطلال
bachelor *a'zab, 'uzaab*	أعزب
advertising (n) *i'laan*	إعلان
above *a'la*	أعلى
blind (adj, without sight) *a'maa*	أعمى
majority *aghlabey-ya*	أغلبية
song *ughneya, aghaani*	أغنية
better *afDal*	أفضل
Afghanistan *afghaanistaan*	أفغانستان
Afghan (adj) *afghaani, afghaan*	أفغاني

landscape (adj, horizontal) *ufuqeyy*	أفقي
accommodation *iqaama*	إقامة
suggestion *iqtiraaH, iqtiraaHaat*	اقتراح
economic; budget (adj, cheaper) *iqtiSaadeyy*	اقتصادي
next of kin *aqrab al-aqribaa'*	أقرب الأقرباء
maximum *aqSaa*	أقصى
less (adj, fewer); least (adj) *aqall*	أقل
province *iqleem, aqaaleem*	إقليم
regional *iqleemee*	إقليمي
more *akthar*	أكثر
tip (n, gratuity) *ikramey-ya, ikramey-yaat*	إكرامية
food *akl*	أكل
Jordan *al-urdunn*	الأردن
elder (n) *al-akbar*	الأكبر
Emirates *al-imaaraat*	الإمارات
labor pains *aalaam al-waD'*	آلام الوضع
United Nations *al-umam al-muttaHida*	الأمم المتحدة
now *al-aan*	الآن
instrument *aala, aalaat*	آلة
laryngitis *iltihaab al-hanjara*	التهاب الحنجرة
Algeria *al-jazaa'ir*	الجزائر
pilgrimage (to Mecca) *al-Hajj*	الحج
fall (n, season) *al-khareef*	الخريف
Casablanca *ad-daar al- bayDaa'*	الدار البيضاء
spring (n, season) *ar-rabee'*	الربيع
Saudi (Arabia) *as-sa'oodey-ya*	السعودية
Sudan *as-soodaan*	السودان
colloquial language *al-'aamey-ya*	العامية
Iraq *al-'iraaq*	العراق
Arabic language *al-'arabeyya*	العربية
cancellation *ilghaa'*	إلغاء
Euphrates *al-furaat*	الفرات
Cairo *al-qaahira*	القاهرة
Kabyle (in Algeria) *al-kabaa'il*	القبائل
Jerusalem *al-quds*	القدس
Koran *al-quraan al-kareem*	القرآن الكريم
alcohol *al-kuHool*	الكحول

earth (planet) *al-kura l-arDey-ya*	الكرة الأرضية
Kaaba (in Mecca) *al-kaa'ba*	الكعبة
Kuwait *al-kuwait*	الكويت
English language *al-lugha al-ingeleezey-ya*	اللغة الانجليزية
Allah; God *al-laah*	الله
tonight *al-laila*	الليلة
pain; ache (n) *alam, aalaam*	ألم
Christianity *al-maseeHey-ya*	المسيحية
Levant *al-mashriq al-'arabi*	المشرق العربي
Morocco *al-maghrib*	المغرب
Nubia *an-nooba*	النوبة
Nile *an-neel*	النيل
down(wards) *ila asfal*	إلى أسفل
until (prep) *ila 'an*	إلى أن
Yemen *al-yaman*	اليمن
today *al-yawm*	اليوم
mother (n) *umm*	أم
forward (adj) *amaameyy*	أمامي
examination (n, school) *imtiHaan, imtiHaanaat*	امتحان
baggage (n) *amti'a*	أمتعة
gratitude (adj) *imtinaan*	امتنان
excellence *imtiyaaz*	امتياز
woman *imra'a, nisaa'*	امرأة
gynecology *amraaD nisaa'*	أمراض نساء.
yesterday *ams*	أمس
constipation *imsaak*	إمساك
security (n) *amn*	أمن
wish (n) *umniya, umniyaat*	أمنية
emir; prince *ameer, umaraa'*	أمير
princess *ameera, ameeraat*	أميرة
I *ana*	أنا
snorkel (n) *unboob at-tanaf-fus*	أنبوب التنفس
uprising *intifaaDa*	انتفاضة
female *untha*	أنثى
England *ingeltera*	انجلترا
English (person) *ingeleezeyy, ingeleez*	انجليزي
bible *injeel*	انجيل

bend (n, contour) *inHinaa'*	انحناء
nose *anf*	أنف
rescue (n) *inqaadh*	إنقاذ
breakdown (n, nervous) *inhiyaar 'aSabeyy*	انهيار عصبي
insult (n) *ihaana, ihaanaat*	إهانة
or *aw*	أو
Europe *orob-baa*	أوروبا
European *orob-beyy, orob-bey-yeen*	أوروبي
sale (n, discount) *okazyon, okazyonaat*	أوكازيون
first *aw-wal*	أول
anybody *ayy shakhS*	أي شخص
anything *ayy shai'*	أي شيء،
anywhere *ayy makaan*	أي مكان
which? *ayy*	أي؟
positive *eejaabee*	ايجابي
Iran *eeraan*	إيران
Iranian *eeraaneyy*	إيراني
receipt *eeSaal, eeSaalaat*	إيصال
also *aiDan*	أيضا
beat (n, tempo, music) *eeqaa'*	إيقاع
icon *ayqoona, ayqoonaat*	أيقونة
faith; belief *'eeman*	إيمان
where? *aina*	أين؟

ب *(baa)*

door *baab, abwaab*	باب
bus *baaS, baaSaat*	باص
Babylon *baabil*	بابل
eggplant *baadhinjaan*	باذنجان
well (n, for water) *bi'r, aabaar*	بئر
cold (adj) *baarid*	بارد
peas *bazilaa'*	بازلاء،
coach (n, bus) *baaS, baaSaat*	باص
void (adj, invalidated) *baaTil*	باطل
mosquito *baa'ooDa, baa'ooD*	باعوضة

across *bil'arD*	بالعرض
okra *bamya*	بامية
veal *bitel-lo*	بتللو
beside *bijaanib*	بجانب
sailor *baH-Haar, baH-Haara*	بحار
sea *baHr*	بحر
marine (adj) *baHreyy*	بحري
Bahrain *al-baHrayn*	البحرين
Bahraini *baHrayneyy*	بحريني
lake *buHaira, buHairaat*	بحيرة
incense (aromatic products) *bukhoor*	بخور
precisely *bi-diq-qa*	بدقة
instead of *badalan 'an*	بدلا عن
bedouin *badaweyy*	بدوي
suit (n, clothing) *badhla*	بذلة
overland *bar-ran*	برا
Berber *barbar*	بربر
orange (n, fruit) *burtuqaala, burtuqaal*	برتقال
orange (adj, color) *burtuqaaleyy*	برتقالي
tower *burj, abraaj*	برج
lightning *barq*	برق
pool (n, pond, etc.) *birka, birak*	بركة
proof *burhaan*	برهان
wild (adj, uncultivated) *bar-reyy*	بري
innocent (adj, not guilty) *baree'*	بريء
mail (n, post) *bareed*	بريد
airmail (n) *bareed jaw-weyy*	بريد جوي
British (adj) *biriTaaneyy, biriTaaney-yeen*	بريطاني
Britain *biriTaanya*	بريطانيا
lozenge pastille *basteelya*	بستيلية
simple *baseeT*	بسيط
eyesight *baSar*	بصر
onion *baSal*	بصل
card *biTaaqa, biTaaqaat*	بطاقة
postcard *biTaqa bareedey-ya*	بطاقة بريدية
charge card *biTaaqat Hisaab*	بطاقة حساب
unemployment (n) *biTaala*	بطالة

blanket *baT-Taney-ya, baTaaTeen*	بطانية
duck (n) *baT-Ta, baTT*	بطة
slow (adj) *baTee'*	بطيء
after (prep) *ba'd*	بعد
afternoon (n) *ba'd aDH-DHuhr*	بعد الظهر
some *baa'D*	بعض
far *ba'eed*	بعيد
grocer *baq-qaal*	بقال
cow *baqara, baqar*	بقرة
spot (n, stain) *buq'a, buqa'*	بقعة
unattended *bilaa riqaaba*	بلا رقابة
date (fruit) *balaHa, balaH*	بلحة
bilingual *bilughatain*	بلغتين
blouse *bilooza*	بلوزة
coffee (beans) *bunn*	بن
building *binaa', abneya*	بناء
girl *bint, banaat*	بنت
niece (daughter of brother) *bint akh*	بنت أخ
niece (daughter of sister) *bint ukht*	بنت أخت
gas (n, petrol) *banzeen*	بنزين
purple *banafsajeyy*	بنفسجي
lavender (n, color) *banafsajeyy faatiH*	بنفسجي فاتح
brown *bun-neyy*	بني
hall *bahw*	بهو
gate *baw-waaba, baw-waabaat*	بوابة
inch *booSa, booSaat*	بوصة
environment *bee'a*	بيئة
linen *bayaDaat*	بياضات
breakdown (n, itemization) *bayaan mufaS-Sal*	بيان مفصل
home; house *bait, buyoot*	بيت
youth hostel *bait ash-shabaab*	بيت الشباب
kennel (n, dog) *bayt al-kalb, buyoot al-kilaab*	بيت الكلب
mansion *bait fakhm, buyoot fakhma*	بيت فخم
Bethlehem *bait laHm*	بيت لحم
beer *beera*	بيرة
bureaucracy *beeroqraTey-ya*	بيروقراطية
egg *baiDa, baiD*	بيضة

veterinary **baiTareyy**	بيطري
between **bain**	بين

ت (taa)

sarcophagus **taaboot Hajareyy**	تابوت حجري
trader **taajir, tuj-jaar**	تاجر
date (day); history **taareekh, tawaareekh**	تاريخ
visa **ta'sheera, ta'sheeraat**	تأشيرة
cab (n) **taksee**	تاكسي
next **taali**	تال
total (adj, entire) **taam**	تام
insurance **ta'meen**	تأمين
restoration **tajdeed**	تجديد
manicure **tajmeel aDHaafir al-yad**	تجميل أظافر اليد
cavity **tajweef**	تجويف
under (prep) **taHt**	تحت
caution (n, warning) **taHdheer**	تحذير
antiques **tuHaf qadeema**	تحف قديمة
masterpiece **tuHfa, tuHaf**	تحفة
embalming (n) **taHneeT**	تحنيط
transfer (n) **taHweel, taHweelaat**	تحويل
greeting (n) **taHey-ya, taHey-yaat**	تحية
camping trip (n) **takhyeem**	تخييم
massage **tadleek**	تدليك
memento **tidhkaar**	تذكار
ticket (n) **tadhkara, tadhaakir**	تذكرة
taste (n, sense) **tadhaw-wuq**	تذوق
dust (n) **turaab**	تراب
consent (n) **taraaDi**	تراض
welcome (n) **tarHeeb**	ترحيب
license **tarkheeS, taraakheeS**	ترخيص
tailor (n) **tarzi, tarzey-ya**	ترزي
upgrade (n) **tarqeya**	ترقية
Turkey **torkeya**	تركيا
lubrication **tazyeet**	تزييت

climb (n) *tasal-luq*	تسلق
entertainment *tasliya*	تسلية
marketing *tasweeq*	تسويق
similarity *tashaabuh*	تشابه
diagnosis *tash-kheeS*	تشخيص
trim (n, hair, etc.) *tash-dheeb*	تشذيب
assortment *tashkeela*	تشكيلة
crash (n) *taSaadum*	تصادم
pass (n, permit) *taSreeH, taSaareeH*	تصريح
repair (n) *taSleeH*	تصليح
vaccination; inoculation *taT'eem*	تطعيم
voluntary (n) *tataw-wu'eyy*	تطوعي
tired (adj) *ta'baan*	تعبان
expression (phrase) *ta'beer, ta'beeraat*	تعبير
breakdown (n, malfunction) *Ta'aT-Tul*	تعطل
education *ta'leem*	تعليم
compensation *ta'weeD*	تعويض
miserable (sad) *ta'ees*	تعيس
change (n, alteration) *taghyeer, taghyeeraat*	تغيير
apple *tufaaHa, tufaaH*	تفاحة
details *tafaaSeel*	تفاصيل
retirement (from work) *taqaa'ud*	تقاعد
customs (n, traditions) *taqaaleed*	تقاليد
estimate (n) *taqdeer*	تقدير
almost *taqreeban*	تقريبا
traditional (adj) *taqleedeyy*	تقليدي
air conditioning (n) *takyeef ul-hawaa'*	تكييف الهواء
hill *tall, tilaal*	تل
damage (n) *talaf*	تلف
statue *timthaal, tamaatheel*	تمثال
exercise (n) *tamreen, tamreenaat*	تمرين
crocodile *timsaaH, tamaaseeH*	تمساح
excavation *tanqeeb*	تنقيب
leak (n) *tanqeeT*	تنقيط
charge (n, accusation) *tuhma*	تهمة
ventilation *tahwiya*	تهوية
spices (n) *tawaabil*	توابل

dressing (n, salad flavoring) *tawaabil as-salaTa*	توابل السلطة
twin *taw'am, tawaa'im*	توأم
recommendation *tawSey-ya*	توصية
signature *tawqee', tawqee'aat*	توقيع
Tunis *toonis*	تونس
Tunisian *tooniseyy, toonisey-yeen*	تونسي
current (electric) *tay-yaar kahrubaa'eyy*	تيار كهربائي
current (water) *tay-yaar maa'eyy*	تيار مائي
fig *teena, teen*	تينة

ث (thaa)

second (n, after first) *thaani*	ثان
second (n, time) *thaanya, thawaani*	ثانية
chit-chat (n) *tharthara*	ثرثرة
hole; puncture *thuqb, thuqoob*	ثقب
keyhole *thuqb al-moftaaH*	ثقب المفتاح
heavy *thaqeel*	ثقيل
fridge *thal-laaja, thal-laajaat*	ثلاجة
ice *thalj*	ثلج
cost (n) *thaman*	ثمن
valuable *thameen*	ثمين
garlic *thawm*	ثوم

ج (jeem)

dry (adj) *jaaf*	جاف
gallon *galoon*	جالون
university *jaami'a, jaami'aat*	جامعة
buffalo *jaamoosa, jaamoos*	جاموسة
ready (adj) *jaahiz*	جاهز
mountain *jabal, jibaal*	جبل
cheese *jubna*	جنة
grandfather *jidd*	جد
serious *jid-deyy*	جدي

new *jadeed*	جديد
attractive *jadh-dhaab*	جذاب
root (n) *jidhr, judhoor*	جذر
germs *jaraatheem*	جراثيم
surgery (n, operation) *jiraaHa, jiraaHaat*	جراحة
wound (n) *jarH, jiraaH*	جرح
rat *jurdh, jurdhaan*	جرذ
doorbell *jaras al-baab*	جرس الباب
waiter (n) *garsoon*	جرسون
dosage *jur'a, jur'aat*	جرعة
newspaper *jareeda, jaraa'id*	جريدة
crime *jareema, jaraa'im*	جريمة
part (n, section) *juz', ajzaa'*	جزء
Algerian *jazaa'ireyy, jazaa'irey≠yeen*	جزائري
butcher (n) *jaz-zaar, jaz-zaareen*	جزار
carrot *jazar*	جزر
island *jazeera, juzur*	جزيرة
bridge (n) *jisr, jusoor*	جسر
body *jism, ajsaam*	جسم
skin (n); leather *jild*	جلد
customs (n, import duties) *jamaarik*	جمارك
shrimp; prawns *gambari* (coll.)	جمبري
camel *jamal, jimaal*	جمل
wholesale *jumla*	جملة
beautiful *jameel*	جميل
wing (n); suite (hotel) *jinaaH, ajniHa*	جناح
soldier (n) *jundeyy, junood*	جندي
ginger (n, herb) *ganzabeel*	جنزبيل
nationality *jinsey-ya, jinsey-yaat*	جنسية
appliance *jihaaz, ajhiza*	جهاز
effort *juhd, juhood*	جهد
weather (n) *jaww*	جو
passport *jawaaz safar*	جواز سفر
guava *jawaafa*	جوافة
quality (n) *jawda*	جودة
hunger (n) *joo'*	جوع
excursion; tour (n) *jawla, jawlaaat*	جولة

cruise (n) *jawla baHrey-ya*	جولة بحرية
skirt *gunel-la, gunel-laat*	جونلة
gem *jawhara, jawaahir*	جوهرة
jeweler *jawharjeyy*	جوهرجي
pocket (n) *jaib, juyoob*	جيب
skirt *jeeba, jeebaat*	جيبة

ح (Haa)

wall *Haa'iT, Hawaa'iT*	حائط
Wailing Wall *Haa'iT al-mabka*	حائط المبكى
pilgrim *Haajj, Hujjaaj*	حاج
eyebrow *Haajib, Hawaajib*	حاجب
need (n) *Haaja, Haajaat*	حاجة
rabbi *Haakhaam*	حاخام
accident *Haadith, Hawaadith*	حادث
hot *Harr*	حار
guard (n); keeper (of park, etc.) *Haaris, Hor-ras*	حارس
hoof *Haafir, Hawaafir*	حافر
wallet *HaafiDHa*	حافظة
case; condition (n) *Haala*	حالة
pregnant *Haamil*	حامل
love (n) *Hubb*	حب
rope *Habl, Hibaal*	حبل
cardamom *Hab-bahaan*	حبهان
breakfast cereal *Huboob al-fuToor*	حبوب الفطور
veil (n) *Hijaab*	حجاب
stone (n) *Hajar, aHjaar*	حجر
room (n, hotel, etc.) *Hujra, Hujraat*	حجرة
reservation (n) *Hajz, Hujuzaat*	حجز
size (n) *Hajm, aHjaam*	حجم
edge; limit *Hadd, Hudood*	حد
minimum charge *Hadd adnaa*	حد أدنى
iron (n, metal) *Hadeed*	حديد
garden; park (n) *Hadeeqa, Hadaa'iq*	حديقة
zoo *Hadeeqat al-Hayawaan*	حديقة الحيوان

shoe *Hidhaa', aHdheya*	حذاء
dialing tone *Haraara*	حرارة (تليفون)
war *Harb*	حرب
letter (alphabet) *Harf, Huroof*	حرف
craftsmanship *Hirafey-ya*	حرفية
sunburn (n) *Hurooq ash-shams*	حروق الشمس
silk (n) *Hareer*	حرير
silk (adj) *Hareereyy*	حريري
party (n, political group) *Hizb, aHzaab*	حزب
Labor Party *Hizb al-'ummaal*	حزب العمال
unhappy; sad *Hazeen*	حزين
account (n, bank) *Hisaab, Hisaabaat*	حساب
current account *Hisaab jaari*	حساب جار
allergic; sensitive *Has-saas*	حساس
good *Hasan*	حسن
insect *Hashra, Hashraat*	حشرة
horse *HiSaan, aHSina*	حصان
measles *HaSba*	حصبة
civilization *HaDaara, HaDaaraat*	حضارة
wreckage *HuTaam*	حطام
luck *HaDH*	حظ
diaper *Haf-faaDa*	حفاضة
party (n, ball) *Hafla, Haflaat*	حفلة
concert (n) *Hafla museeqey-ya*	حفلة موسيقية
grandchild *Hafeed, aHfaad*	حفيد
right (n, entitlement) *Haqq, Huqooq*	حق
syringe (n); jab *Huqna, Huqan*	حقنة
bag (n) *Haqeeba, Haqaa'ib*	حقيبة
handbag *Haqeebat yad*	حقيبة يد
fact *Haqeeqa, Haqaa'iq*	حقيقة
real; true *Haqeeqeyy*	حقيقي
itching *Hak-ka*	حكة
solution (n, answer) *Hall, Hulool*	حل
compromise (n) *Hall wasaT*	حل وسط
barber *Hal-laaq, Hal-laaqeen*	حلاق
dream (n) *Hilm, aHlaam*	حلم
sweet (adj) *Hulw*	حلو

candy	*Halwaa*	حلوى
milk	*Haleeb*	حليب
donkey	*Himaar, Hameer*	حمار
zebra	*Himaar waH-sheyy*	حمار وحشي
porter	*Ham-maal, Ham-maaleen*	حمال
bathroom	*Ham-maam*	حمام
chickpeas	*Hum-muS*	حمص
lamb (young sheep)	*Hamal*	حمل
load (n)	*Himl, aHmaal*	حمل
father-in-law	*Hamw*	حمو
acidity	*HumooDa*	حموضة
fever	*Hum-maa*	حمى
henna	*Henaa'*	حناء
faucet	*Hanafey-ya, Hanafey-yaat*	حنفية
sink (n)	*HawD, aHwaaD*	حوض
around	*Hawl*	حول
alive; live (adj, wire, etc.)	*Hayy*	حي
commercial district	*Hayy tijaareyy*	حي تجاري
life	*Hayaa*	حياة
animal	**Hayawaan, Hayawaanaat**	حيوان

خ (khaa)

afraid	*khaa'if*	خائف
maid	**khadima, khadimaat**	خادمة
exterior	*khaarijeyy*	خارجي
private	*khaaS*	خاص
equestrian (adj)	*khaaS bil-furoosey-ya*	خاص بالفروسية
wrong (adj)	*khaaTi'*	خاطئ
uncle (maternal)	*khaal, khilaan*	خال
aunt (maternal)	*khaala, khaalaat*	خالة
lean (adj, meat, etc.)	*khaali ad-dihin*	خالي الدهن
news	*khabar, akhbaar*	خبر
experience (n)	*khibra, khibraat*	خبرة
bread	*khubz*	خبز
circumcision	*khitaan*	ختان

service (n, favor) *khidma, khidmaat*	خدمة
khedive *khudaywee*	خديوي
myth *khuraafa, khurafaat*	خرافة
junk *khurda*	خردة
knick-knacks *khurdawaat*	خردوات
artichoke *kharshoof (coll.)*	خرشوف
graduate (adj) *khir-reej*	خريج
map *khareeTa, kharaa'iT*	خريطة
closet *khazaanat malaabis*	خزانة ملابس
safe (n, secure box) *khazna, khizan*	خزنة
lettuce *khass*	خس
loss *khusaara*	خسارة
wood (n, timber) *khashab, akh-shaab*	خشب
beech (wood) *khashab az-zaan*	خشب الزان
rough (adj, not smooth) *khashin*	خشن
waist *khaSr*	خصر
rebate; discount (n) *khaSm, khuSumaat*	خصم
vegetable(s) *khuDaar*	خضار
line *khaTT, khuTooT*	خط
route (n) *khaTT sair*	خط سير
error *khaTa', akhTaa'*	خطأ
letter (mail) *khiTaab*	خطاب
hazard *khaTar*	خطر
dangerous *khaTir*	خطر
engagement (n, for marriage) *khuTooba*	خطوبة
step (n) *khaTwa, khaTwaat*	خطوة
fiancé (male) *khaTeeb*	خطيب
fiancée (female) *khaTeeba*	خطيبة
critical (adj, dangerous) *khaTeer*	خطير
light (adj, opp. heavy); mild *khafeef*	خفيف
vinegar *khall*	خل
during (prep); through (prep) *khilaal*	خلال
bangle *khal-khaal, khalaa-kheel*	خلخال
extraction (n, tooth, etc.) *khal'*	خلع
behind *khalf*	خلف
back (adj, rear) *khalfeyy*	خلفي
fault (n) *khalal*	خلل

gulf *khaleej*	خليج
blend; mixture *khaleeT*	خليط
caliph *khaleefa, kholafaa'*	خليفة
yeast *khameera*	خميرة
dagger *khanjar, khanaajir*	خنجر
fear (n) *khawf*	خوف
cucumber *khiyaar*	خيار
bamboo (n) *khaizaraan*	خيزران
canvas *khaish*	خيش
string (cord) *khaiT, khuyooT*	خيط
tent *khaima, khiyaam*	خيمة

د *(daal)*

kleptomania *daa' as-sirqa*	داء السرقة
circle (n) *daa'ira, dawaa'ir*	دائرة
constant *daa'im*	دائم
always *daa'iman*	دائما
inside *daakhil*	داخل
interior (adj) *daakhileyy*	داخلي
house *daar, diyaar*	دار
warm (adj) *daafi'*	دافئ
hornet *dab-boor, dabaabeer*	دبور
pin (n) *dab-boos, dabaabees*	دبوس
chicken *dajaaj*	دجاج
impostor *daj-jaal, daj-jaaleen*	دجال
smoke (n) *dokh-khaan*	دخان
intruder *dakheel, dukhalaa'*	دخيل
bicycle *dar-raaja, dar-raajaat*	دراجة
degree; extent *daraja, darajaat*	درجة
temperature *darajat al-Haraara*	درجة الحرارة
lesson *dars, duroos*	درس
dolphin *darfeel, daraafeel*	درفيل
dervish *darweesh, daraaweesh*	درويش
dozen *dasta*	دستة
shower (n) *dush*	دش

flour *daqeeq*	دقيق
minute (n, time) *daqeeqa, daqaa'iq*	دقيقة
guidebook *daleel*	دليل
manual (n, booklet) *daleel maTboo'*	دليل مطبوع
blood (n) *dam*	دم
Damascus *dimashq*	دمشق
tear (n, drop) *dam'a, dumoo'*	دمعة
doll *dumya, dumyaat*	دمية
lace (n) *dantella*	دنتلة
fat (n) *duhn*	دهن
medicine; drug (medication) *dawaa', adweya*	دواء
worm *dooda, dood*	دودة
carafe *dawraq, dawaariq*	دورق
country (n, state) *dawla*	دولة
international *duwaleyy*	دولي
monastery, abbey *dair, adyira*	دير
turkey *deek roomeyy*	ديك رومي
religion *deen, adyaan*	دين

ذ (dhaal)

same (adj) *dhaatuh*	ذاته
fly (n, insect) *dhobaaba, dhobaab*	ذبابة
arm (n, anatomical) *dhiraa'*	ذراع
maize *Dhur-ra*	ذرة
male *dhakar, dhukoor*	ذكر
memories *dhikrayaat*	ذكريات
round-trip *dhihaab wa 'awda*	ذهاب وعودة
gold (n) *dhahab*	ذهب

ر (raay)

smell (n, scent) *raa'iHa, rawaa'iH*	رائحة
terrific *raa'i*	رائع
lung *ri'a*	رئة

head (n, anatomy) *ra's, ru'oos*	رأس
adult *raashid, raashideen*	راشد
passenger *raakib, ruk-kaab*	راكب
view (n, opinion) *ra'yy, aaraa'*	رأي
main (adj, central) *ra'eeseyy*	رئيسي
shoelace *ribaaT al-hizhaa'*	رباط الحذاء
quarter (n) *rub'*	ربع
maybe *rub-bama*	ربما
asthma *rabu*	ربو
man *rajul, rijaal*	رجل
leg *rijl, arjul*	رجل
nomad *raH'Haal*	رحال
journey; trip (n, voyage) *riHla, riHlaaat*	رحلة
flight (n, air journey) *riHlat Tayaraan*	رحلة طيران
departure *raHeel*	رحيل
marble (n, stone) *rukhaam*	رخام
inexpensive; cheap *rakheeS*	رخيص
reply (n) *radd, rudood*	رد
rice *ruzz*	رز
message *risaala*	رسالة
formal (adj) *rasmee*	رسمي
prophet *rasool*	رسول
grace (n, elegance) *rashaaqa*	رشاقة
Rosetta *rasheed*	رشيد
lead (n, metal) *ruSaaS*	رصاص
platform (n, for train) *raSeef, arSifa*	رصيف
satisfaction *riDaa*	رضا
humidity *ruTooba*	رطوبة
lather *raghwa*	رغوة
loaf (n, bread) *ragheef, arghifa*	رغيف
companion *rafeeq, rifaaq*	رفيق
neck *raqba*	رقبة
number *raqm, arqaam*	رقم
delicate *raqeeq*	رقيق
knee *rukba, rukab*	ركبة
corner (n) *rukn, arkaan*	ركن
riding (n) *rukoob al-khail*	ركوب الخيل

cycling *rukoob ad-dar-raajaat*	ركوب الدراجات
pomegranate *rum-maan*	رمان
eyelash *rimsh, rumoosh*	رمش
Ramadan *ramaDaan*	رمضان
sand (n) *raml, rimaal*	رمل
bet (n) *rahaan, rahaanaat*	رهان
prescription *rooshet-ta*	روشتة
kindergarten *rawDat aTfaal*	روضة أطفال
khamsin winds *riyaaH al-khamaaseen*	رياح الخماسين
sport (n) *riyaaDa*	رياضة
athletic *riyaaDeyy*	رياضي
mathematics *riyaaDiyaat*	رياضيات
wind (n) *reeH, reeyaaH*	ريح
basil *reeHaan*	ريحان
countryside *reef*	ريف
provincial; rustic *reefeyy*	ريفي

ز (zaay)

angle (n) *zaawiya, zawaayaa*	زاوية
yogurt *zabaadee*	زبادي
trash (n); litter *zibaala*	زبالة
butter *zubd*	زبد
client *zuboon, zabaa'in*	زبون
raisin *zibeeb*	زبيب
glass (n, for mirrors, etc.) *zujaaj*	زجاج
windscreen *zujaaj amaameyy*	زجاج أمامي
bottle (n, glass container) *zujaaja, zujaajaat*	زجاجة
ornamental *zukhrufi*	زخرفي
button (n) *zirr*	زر
agriculture (n) *ziraa'a*	زراعة
thyme *za'tar*	زعتر
saffron *za'faraan*	زعفران
down (n, feathers) *zaghab*	زغب
wedding (n) *zifaaf*	زفاف
emerald (n) *zumur-rud*	زمرد

time (n, eras, etc.) **zaman**	زمن
rose **zahra, zuhoor**	زهرة
marriage **zawaaj**	زواج
husband **zawj, azwaaj**	زوج
wife **zawja, zawjaat**	زوجة
throat **zawr**	زور
launch (n, motorboat) **zawraq saree'**	زورق سريع
visit (n) **ziyaara, ziyaaraat**	زيارة
oil **zait, zuyoot**	زيت
olive **zaitoona, zaitoon**	زيتونة

س (seen)

misunderstanding **soo' fahm**	سوء فهم
tourist (n) **saa'iH, suyaaH**	سائح
driver **saa'iq, saa'iqeen**	سائق
liquid **saa'il, sawaa'il**	سائل
question (n) **su'aal, as'ila**	سؤال
coast (n, shore) **saaHil, sawaaHil**	ساحل
hour **saa'a, sa'aat**	ساعة
watch (n, on wrist) **saa'at yad**	ساعة يد
calm (adj) **saakin**	ساكن
bygone **saalif**	سالف
race (n, running, etc.) **sibaaq, sibaaqaat**	سباق
plumber **sab-baak**	سباك
reason; cause (n) **sabab, asbaab**	سبب
rosary **sibHa**	سبحة
curtain; screen **sitaar**	ستار
carpet (n); rug **sij-jaada, sij-jaad**	سجادة
mat **sij-jaada Sagheera**	سجادة صغيرة
sausages **sujuq**	سجق
prison; jail (n) **sijn, sujoon**	سجن
lizard **siHliyya, saHaali**	سحلية
heat (n) **sukhoona**	سخونة
dam **sadd, sudood**	سد
plug (n) **sad-daada**	سدادة

secret (n); mystery *sirr, asraar*	سر
mirage *saraab*	سراب
saddle (n) *sarj*	سرج
catacomb *sirdaab, saraadeeb*	سرداب
speed (n) *sur'a*	سرعة
burglary *sariqa, sariqaat*	سرقة
joy *suroor*	سرور
secret (adj) *sir-reyy*	سري
bed *sareer, asir-ra*	سرير
quick; fast *saree'*	سريع
inflammable *saree' l-ishti'aal*	سريع الاشتعال
cough (n) *su'aal*	سعال
price (n) *si'r, as'aar*	سعر
youth price *s'ir ash-shabaab*	سعر الشباب
Saudi (Arabian) *sa'oodeyy, sa'oodey-yeen*	سعودي
happy *sa'eed*	سعيد
embassy *sifaara, sifaaraat*	سفارة
ambassador *safeer, sufaraa'*	سفير
ship (n) *safeena, sufun*	سفينة
ceiling; roof *saqf, suqoof*	سقف
railroad *sikka Hadeed*	سكة حديد
sugar (n) *suk-kar*	سكر
intoxicated (adj) *sakraan, sakaara*	سكران
residential *sakaneyy*	سكني
knife (n) *sik-keen, sakaakeen*	سكين
breed (n) *sulaala, sulaalaat*	سلالة
peace *salaam*	سلام
basket *sal-la*	سلة
sultan *sulTaan*	سلطان
cable (n) *silk, aslaak*	سلك
ladder *sil-lim, salaalim*	سلم
descendant *saleel*	سليل
sky *samaa', samawaat*	سماء
broker *simsaar, samaasira*	سمسار
fish (n) *samak*	سمك
shark *samakat al-qirsh*	سمكة القرش
thick *sameek*	سميك

age (n) *sinn*	سن
hump (n, camel's back) *sanaam*	سنام
year *sana, sanawaat*	سنة
tooth *sin-na, asnaan*	سنة
yearly *sanaweyy*	سنوي
oversight *sahw*	سهو
bracelet *siwaar*	سوار
Sudanese *soodaaneyy, soodaaney-yeen*	سوداني
Syrian *sureyy, surey-yeen*	سوري
Syria *surey-yaa*	سوريا
fly (n, zipper) *sosta, sosat*	سوستة
will (auxiliary verb) *sawfa*	سوف
market (n) *sooq, aswaaq*	سوق
shopping mall *sooq mol*	سوق مول
vulgar *sooqeyy*	سوقي
unlucky (adj) *say-yi' al-HaDH*	سي، الحظ
car; vehicle *say-yaara, say-yaaraat*	سيارة
lady *sayyeda, sayyedaat*	سيدة
flush (n) *seefon*	سيفون

ش *(sheen)*

pale (adj) *shaaHib*	شاحب
truck (n); lorry *shaaHina, shaaHinaaat*	شاحنة
beach *shaaTi', shawaaTi'*	شاطئ
thankful (adj) *shaakir*	شاكر
current affairs *shu'oon as-saa'a*	شؤون الساعة
tea (n) *shaay*	شاي
window *shub-baak, shabaabeek*	شباك
slippers *shibshib, shabaashib*	شبشب
web *shabaka*	شبكة
retina *shabakey-ya*	شبكية
winter *shitaa'*	شتاء
tree *shajara, ashjaar*	شجرة
cedar (n) *shajarat al-arz*	شجرة الأرز
shipment (n) *shuHna, shuHnaat*	شحنة

person **shakhS, ash-khaaS**	شخص
sail (n) **shiraa'**	شراع
condition (n, stipulation) **sharT, shurooT**	شرط
balcony; terrace **shurfa, shurfaat**	شرفة
east (n) **sharq**	شرق
eastern; oriental **sharqeyy**	شرقي
company (n, business unit) **sharika, sharikaat**	شركة
bay **sharm**	شرم
sunrise **shorooq**	شروق
artery **shiryaan, sharaayeen**	شريان
slice (n) **shareeHa, sharaa'iH**	شريحة
partner (n) **shareek, shurakaa'**	شريك
coral **shi'aab marjaaney-ya**	شعاب مرجانية
popular **sha'bee**	شعبي
hair **sha'r**	شعر
malt **sha'eer**	شعير
lip **shifaah**	شفاه
verbal **shafaweyy**	شفوي
apartment **shiq-qa, shuqaq**	شقة
doubt (n) **shakk**	شك
shape (n) **shakl, ashkaal**	شكل
waterfall **shal-laal, shal-laalaat**	شلال
smell (n, sense) **shamm**	شم
north **shamaal**	شمال
melon **sham-maam**	شمام
sun (n) **shams**	شمس
wax (n) **sham'**	شمع
candle **sham'a, shimoo'**	شمعة
university degree **shihaada jaame'ey-ya**	شهادة جامعية
month **shahr, shuhoor**	شهر
monthly **shahreyy**	شهري
gallant **shahm**	شهم
soup **shorba**	شوربة
fork **shawka, shuwak**	شوكة
thing **shai', ashyaa'**	شيء
sheik **shaikh, shuyookh**	شيخ
hookah; water pipe **sheesha**	شيشة

devil **shayTaan, shayaaTeen**	شيطان
blank check **sheek 'ala bayaaD**	شيك على بياض
traveler's checks **sheekaat seyaaHey-ya**	شيكات سياحية
rye (n) **shailam**	شيلم

(Saad) ص

soap (n) **Saaboon**	صابون
clear (adj, unclouded) **Saafi**	صاف
hotel lobby **Saalat al-funduq**	صالة الفندق
valid **SaaliH**	صالح
locksmith **Saani' aqfaal**	صانع أقفال
morning **SabaaH**	صباح
cactus **Sab-baar**	صبار
patience (n) **Sabr**	صبر
juvenile (adj) **Sibyaaneyy**	صبياني
press (n, magazines, etc.) **SaHaafa**	صحافة
journalist **SaHaafeyy, SaHafey-yeen**	صحافي
health **SiH-Ha**	صحة
desert (n) **SaHraa'**	صحراء
reporter **SaHafee, SaHafeeyeen**	صحفي
plate (n, dish) **saHn, SuHoon**	صحن
sanitary **SiH-Heyy**	صحي
right (correct) **saHeeH**	صحيح
rock **Sakhra, Sokhoor**	صخرة
reef **Sukhoor baHrey-ya**	صخور بحرية
headache **Sodaa'**	صداع
migraine **Sudaa' niSfeyy**	صداع نصفي
breast **Sadr, Sudoor**	صدر
chance **Sudfa**	صدفة
charity (n, donation) **Sadaqa, Sadaqaat**	صدقة
shock (n) **Sadma, Sadmaat**	صدمة
friend **Sadeeq, aSdiqaa'**	صديق
epilepsy (n) **Sara'**	صرع
frank (honest) **SareeH**	صريح
difficult **Sa'b**	صعب

little; small *Sagheer* صغير

young (adj) *sagheer as-sinn* صغير السن

zero *Sifr* صفر

hepatitis *Safraa'* صفراء

bargain (n) *Safqa, Safqaat* صفقة

falcon; hawk *Saqr, Suqoor* صقر

cross (n, crucifix) *Saleeb* صليب

silence (n) *Samt* صمت

sound (n); voice (n) *Sawt, aSwaat* صوت

picture (n, photo, etc.) *Soora, Suwar* صورة

wool *Soof, aSwaaf* صوف

fast (n) *Sawm* صوم

Lent *Siyaam al-maseeHey-yeen* صيام المسيحيين

maintenance (servicing) *Siyaana* صيانة

pharmacy *Saydaley-ya, Saydaley-yaat* صيدلية

summer *Saif* صيف

ض (Daad)

officer (military) *DaabiT, Dub-baaT* ضابط

lamb (meat) *Daanee Sagheer* ضاني صغير

fog *Dabaab* ضباب

noise *Dajeej* ضجيج

laughter *DaHik* ضحك

massive *Dakhm* ضخم

against *Didd* ضد

knock out (n, in boxing) *Darba qaaDey-ya* ضربة قاضية

harm (n) *Darar* ضرر

essential; necessary *Darooreyy* ضروري

tax (n) *Dareeba, Daraa'ib* ضريبة

mausoleum; shrine *DareeH, aDreHa* ضريح

weak *Da'eef* ضعيف

credit (n); warranty *Damaan* ضمان

light (n, sunlight, etc.) *Daw', aDwaa'* ضوء

headlights *Daw' 'aali* ضوء، عال

guest (n) *Daif, Duyoof* ضيف

narrow; tight *Day-yiq*	ضيق
company (n, guests) *Duycof*	ضيوف

ط (Taa)

bird *Taa'ir, Tiyoor*	طائر
airplane *Taa'ira, Taa'iraat*	طائرة
wild (adj, reckless) *Taa'ish*	طائش
stamp (n, postage) *Taabi' bareed*	طابع بريد
story (n, level) *Taabiq, Tawaabiq*	طابق
windmill *TaaHoona, TawaaHeen*	طاحونة
repellent (n) *Taarid*	طارد
fresh *Taazij*	طازج
student (n) *Taalib, Talaba*	طالب
undergraduate *Taalib fee l-jaami'a*	طالب في الجامعة
backgammon *Tawlit az-zahr*	طاولة الزهر
cook (n, chef) *Tab-baakh, Tab-baakheen*	طباخ
dish (n) *Tabaq, aTbaaq*	طبق
dessert *Tabaq al-Hilw*	طبق الحلو
layer (n) *Tabaqa, Tabaqaat*	طبقة
medical *Tib-beyy*	طبي
dentist *Tabeeb asnaan*	طبيب أسنان
natural *Tabi'eyy*	طبيعي
style (n); make (n, brand, etc.) *Tiraaz, Tiraazaat*	طراز
fez *Tarboosh*	طربوش
package (n) *Tard, Turood*	طرد
soft *Tareyy*	طري
quaint *Tareef*	طريف
road; way (n, route) *Tareeq, Turuq*	طريق
cul-de-sac *Tareeq masdood*	طريق مسدود
way (n, method) *Tareeqa, Turuq*	طريقة
rash (n) *TafH jildee*	طفح جلدي
child; infant *Tifl, aTfaal*	طفل
parasite *Tofaileyy*	طفيلي
set (n, specific group) *Taqm, aTqum*	طقم
dentures *Taqm asnaan*	طقم أسنان

divorce (n) *Talaaq*	طلاق
request (n) *Talab, Talabaat*	طلب
loose (adj, free) *Taleeq*	طليق
tomato *TamaaTim*	طماطم
emergency (n) *Tawaari'*	طوارئ
lifebuoy *Tawq an-najaah, atwaaq an-najaah*	طوق النجاة
length *Tool*	طول
long (adj, lengthy) *Taweel*	طويل
kind (adj, good-natured) *Tay-yib*	طيب

ظ (DHaa)

shade (n, from sun, etc.) *DHil, DHilaal*	ظل
back (n, anatomical) *DHahr, DHuhoor*	ظهر

ع ('ain)

ivory *'aaj*	عاج
fair (just) *'aadil*	عادل
just (adj, fair) *'aadil*	عادل
exhaust (n, fumes) *'aadim*	عادم
normal; ordinary *'aadeyy*	عادي
condom *'aazil Tib-beyy, 'awaazil Tib-bey-ya*	عازل طبي
storm (n) *'aaSifa, 'awaaSif*	عاصفة
capital (city) *'aaSima, 'awaaSim*	عاصمة
high (tall) *aali*	عال
world *'aalam*	عالم
loud *'aali aS-Sawt*	عالي الصوت
ancient *'ateeq*	عتيق
disability *'ajz*	عجز
wheel *ajala, ajalaat*	عجلة
dough *'ajeen*	عجين
justice (n) *'adaala*	عدالة
lentils *'ads*	عدس
lens *adasa, adasaat*	عدسة

excuse (n) *'udhr, a'dhaar*	عذر
Iraqi *'iraaqeyy, iraaqey-yeen*	عراقي
Arab(ian) *'arabee*	عربي
performance; show (n); offer (n) *'arD, 'urooD*	عرض
bride *'aroosa, 'araa'is*	عروسة
bridegroom *'arees, 'irsaan*	عريس
wide *'areeD*	عريض
indigestion *'usr haDm*	عسر هضم
military (adj) *'askaree*	عسكري
honey *'asal*	عسل
dinner *'ashaa'*	عشاء
herb *'ushb, a'shaab*	عشب
nerve *'aSab, a'Saab*	عصب
modern *'aSree*	عصري
muscle *'aDala, 'aDalaat*	عضلة
organic *'uDwee*	عضوي
membership (n) *'uDwey-ya*	عضوية
thirsty *'atshaan*	عطشان
vacation; holiday; leave (n) *'uTla, 'uTlaat*	عطلة
bone *'aDHma, 'iDHaam*	عظمة
great (adj, marvelous) *'aDHeem*	عظيم
pardon (n, amnesty) *'afw*	عفو
knot *'uqda*	عقدة
carnelian *'aqeeq aHmar*	عقيق أحمر
reverse (n); opposite *'aks*	عكس
therapy; remedy; cure (n) *'ilaaj*	علاج
relationship *'ilaaqa, 'ilaaqaat*	علاقة
sign (n, mark) *'alaama, 'alaamaat*	علامة
box (n) *'ulba, 'ulab*	علبة
match-box **ulbat kibreet**	علبة كبريت
Egyptology *'ilm al-miSrey-yaat*	علم المصريات
on *'ala*	على
uncle (paternal) *'amm, 'amaam*	عم
Oman *'umaan*	عمان
Omani *'umaaneyy, umaaney-yeen*	عماني
aunt (paternal) *'am-ma, am-maat*	عمة
mayor *'umda, 'umad*	عمدة

work (n, job) *'amal*	عمل
currency *'umla, 'umlaat*	عملة
operation *'amaley-ya, 'amaley-yaat*	عملية
commission (fee) *'umoola, 'umoolaat*	عمولة
deep (adj) *'ameeq*	عميق
care (n) *'inaaya*	عناية
grape *'inaba, 'inab*	عنبة
ambergris *'anbar*	عنبر
ward (hospital) *'anbar, 'anaabir*	عنبر
goat *'anza, anzaat*	عنزة
address (n, street) *'unwaan, 'anaaween*	عنوان
rubber ring *'aw-waama*	عوامة
return (n) *'awda*	عودة
surgery (n, clinic) *'iyaada, 'iyaadaat*	عيادة
feast (n) *'eed, a'yaad*	عيد
Labor Day *'eed al-'ummaal*	عيد العمال
Easter *eed al-fiSH*	عيد الفصح
birthday *'eed milaad*	عيد ميلاد
eye (n, anatomical) *'ain, 'uyoon*	عين
sample (n, small example) *'ay-yina, 'ay-yinaat*	عينة

غ (ghain)

absent *ghaa'ib*	غائب
angry *ghaaDib*	غاضب
expensive *ghali*	غال
vague (adj) *ghaamiD*	غامض
tomorrow *ghadan*	غدا
lunch *ghadaa'*	غداء
gland *ghud-da, ghud-dad*	غدة
fine (n) *gharaama, gharaamaat*	غرامة
west *gharb*	غرب
vacancy (in hotel) *ghuraf khaaliya*	غرف خالية
theater (n, in hospital) *ghurfat al-'amaley-yaat*	غرفة العمليات
bedroom *ghurfat nawm*	غرفة نوم
sunset *ghoroob*	غروب

strange; funny (peculiar) *ghareeb*	غريب
deer; gazelle *ghazaal, ghuzlaan*	غزال
yarn (n, thread) *ghazl*	غزل
dishwasher *ghas-saalat aTbaaq*	غسالة أطباق
washing machine *ghas-saalat malaabis*	غسالة ملابس
laundry (n, clothes, etc.) *ghaseel*	غسيل
angry; cross *ghaDbaan, ghaDbaaneen*	غضبان
cover (n, lid) *ghaTaa', aghTey-ya*	غطاء
scuba diving (n) *ghaTs*	غطس
kettle *ghallaayat al-maa'*	غلاية الماء
mistake (n) *ghalTa, ghalaTaat*	غلطة
wealthy *ghaneyy*	غني
diving, scuba (n) *ghawS*	غوص
unofficial *ghair rasmeyy*	غير رسمي
unhealthy *ghair SiH-Hi*	غير صحي
incorrect *ghair saHeeH*	غير صحيح
unable *ghair qaadir*	غير قادر
illegal *ghair qaanooneyy*	غير قانوني
uncommon *ghair ma'loof*	غير مألوف
uncomfortable *ghair mureeH*	غير مريح
unreasonable *ghair ma'qool*	غير معقول
unsuitable *ghair munaasib*	غير مناسب
uncertain *ghair waathiq*	غير واثق

(faa) ف

benefit (n); use (n) *faa'ida, fawaa'id*	فائدة
check (n, bill) *fatoora, fawaateer*	فاتورة
empty; blank *faarigh*	فارغ
bad, rotten *faasid*	فاسد
green beans *faSolya*	فاصوليا
indecent *faaDiH*	فاضح
fruit *faakiha, fawaakih*	فاكهة
lantern *fanoos, fawaanees*	فانوس
dawn (n) *fajr*	فجر
examination (n, medical) *faHS, fuHooSaat*	فحص

blood test *faHS dam*	فحص دم
pottery *fukh-khaar*	فخار
luxurious *fakhm*	فخم
strawberry *farawla*	فراولة
paradise *firdaws*	فردوس
mare *farasa, farasaat*	فرسة
opportunity *furSa, furaS*	فرصة
Pharaonic *fir'awneyy*	فرعوني
difference *farq, furooq*	فرق
oven *furn*	فرن
scalp (n) *farwat ar-ra's*	فروة الرأس
prey *fareesa*	فريسة
dress (n, clothing item) *fustaan, fasaateen*	فستان
season (n, spring, etc.) *faSl, fuSool*	فصل
blood group *faSeelat ad-dam*	فصيلة الدم
silver (n) *faD-Da*	فضة
silver (adj) *faD-Deyy*	فضي
breakfast *fuToor*	فطور
terrible *faDHee'*	فظيع
effective *fa'aal*	فعال
only; just *faqaT*	فقط
jaw *fakk*	فك
change (n, coins) *fak-ka*	فكة
idea *fikra, afkaar*	فكرة
Palestine *falasTeen*	فلسطين
Palestinian *falasTeeneyy, falasTeeney-yeen*	فلسطيني
pepper (n) *filfil*	فلفل
astronomical *falakeyy*	فلكي
mouth *fam*	فم
art *fann*	فن
calligraphy *fann al-khaTT*	فن الخط
lighthouse *fanaara*	فنارة
artist *fannaan, fannaaneen*	فنان
cup (n, for drinks) *finjaan, fanajeen*	فنجان
hotel *funduq, fanaadiq*	فندق
appetizers *fawaatiH ash-shahey-ya*	فواتح الشهية
immediate *fawreyy*	فوري

mess (n, chaos) *fawDa*	فوضى
up *fawq*	فوق
fava beans *fool*	فول
in *fee*	في
unconscious *fee ighmaa'a*	في إغماءة
outside *fil-khaarij*	في الخارج
elephant *feel, afyaal*	فيل
movie *film, aflaam*	فيلم

ق (qaaf)

leader (n, chief) *qaa'id, qaada*	قائد
menu; list (n) *qaa'ima, qawaa'im*	قائمة
lifeboat *qaarib an-najaah, qawaarib an-najaah*	قارب النجاة
magistrate *qaaDi aw-wal*	قاض أول
lounge (n) *qaa'at jiloos, qaa'aat jiloos*	قاعة جلوس
dictionary *qaamoos, qawaamees*	قاموس
law *qaanoon, qawaaneen*	قانون
legal *qanooneyy*	قانوني
dome *qub-ba, qibaab*	قبة
Copt (n) *qibTeyy, aqbaaT*	قبطي
hat *quba'a*	قبعة
before *qabl*	قبل
kiss (n) *qubla, qublaat*	قبلة
tribe *qabeela, qabaa'il*	قبيلة
mass (church service) *qud-daas*	قداس
foot *qadam, aqdaam*	قدم
able *qadeer*	قدير
saint *qid-dees, qid-deeseen*	قديس
old (object) *qadeem*	قديم
dirty (adj) *qadhir*	قذر
ulcer *qurHa*	قرحة
pill *qurS, aqraaS*	قرص
tablet *qurS, aqraaS*	قرص
loan (n) *qarD, qurooD*	قرض
rural *qaraweyy*	قروي

near *qareeb*	قريب
relative (n) *qareeb, aqaarib*	قريب
village *qarya, quraa*	قرية
station (n, police) *qism al-bolees*	قسم البوليس
zest (n, lemon); plate (gold, etc.) *qishra*	قشرة
story (n, tale) *qiS-Sa, qiSaS*	قصة
palace *qaSr, quSoor*	قصر
short (adj, opp. long) *qaSeer*	قصير
case (n, court) *qaDey-ya*	قضية
train (n) *qiTaar, qiTaaraa*	قطار
cat *qiT-Ta, qiTaT*	قطة
Qatar *qaTar*	قطر
Qatari *qaTareyy, qaTarey-yeen*	قطري
piece (n) *qiT'a, qiTa'*	قطعة
cotton (n) *quTn*	قطن
velvet *qaTeefa*	قطيفة
leap (n) *qafza, qafzaat*	قفزة
lock (n); padlock (n) *qifl, aqfaal*	قفل
heart *qalb, quloob*	قلب
castle; citadel; fortress *qal'a, qilaa'*	قلعة
uneasy; concerned; worried *qaliq*	قلق
pencil *qalam ruSaaS*	قلم رصاص
few (adj) *qaleel*	قليل
gambling *qumaar*	قمار
fabric; material *qumaash, aqmisha*	قماش
wheat *qamH*	قمح
moon *qamar, aqmaar*	قمر
satellite *qamar Sinaa'eyy*	قمر صناعي
lunar *qamareyy*	قمري
shirt (n) *qameeS, qumSaan*	قميص
canal (n, channel) *qanaah, qanawaat*	قناة
mask (n) *qinaa', aqni'a*	قناع
jellyfish *qandeel al-baHr*	قنديل البحر
consulate *qunSuley-ya, qunSuley-yaat*	قنصلية
coffee (beverage) *qahwa*	قهوة
black coffee (no sugar) *qahwa saada*	قهوة سادة
strength *quw-wa, quw-waat*	قوة

strong *qaweyy*	قوي
measurement; fitting (n, trying on) *qiyaas*	قياس
worth (n) *qeema*	قيمة

ك *(kaaf)*

cabin (n) *kabeena, kabaa'in*	كابينة
untrue *kaadhib*	كاذب
phonecard *kart at-tilifon*	كارت التليفون
cup (n, trophy) *ka's, ku'oos*	كأس
khaki (n, color) *kaakee*	كاكي
full; perfect; whole *kaamil*	كامل
kebob *kabaab*	كباب
liver *kabid*	كبد
matches *kibreet*	كبريت
knob (n, of butter, etc.) *kabsha, kabshaat*	كبشة
big; large *kabeer*	كبير
book (n, novel, etc.) *kitaab, kutub*	كتاب
ketchup *kitshab*	كتشب
shoulder (n) *katif, aktaaf*	كتف
pamphlet *kutay-yib*	كتيب
many; plenty *katheer*	كثير
dense *katheef*	كثيف
kohl *koHl*	كحل
tie (n, neck) *karavatta*	كرافتة
ball (n) *kura, kuraat*	كرة
soccer *kurat al-qadam*	كرة القدم
Kurd *kurdeyy, akraad*	كردي
cherries *karz*	كرز
chair; seat (n) *kurseyy, karaasee*	كرسي
celery *karafs*	كرفس
hospitality *karam aD-Diyaafa*	كرم الضيافة
generous *kareem*	كريم
fracture (n) *kasr*	كسر
saucepan *kasarol-la*	كسرولة
lazy *kasool, kasaala*	كسول

kiosk *kushk, akshaak*	كشك
newsstand *kushk al-jaraa'id*	كشك الجرائد
palm (n, anatomy) *kaff*	كف
enough *kifaaya*	كفاية
all; each ;every *kull*	كل
dog *kalb, kilaab*	كلب
word *kalima, kalimaat*	كلمة
kidney *kilya*	كلية
college *kul-ley-ya, kul-ley-yaat*	كلية
sleeve (n) *kumm, akmaam*	كم
quantity; amount *kam-mey-ya, kam-mey-yaat*	كمية
church *kaneesa, kanaa'is*	كنيسة
such *ka-haazha*	كهذا
electricity *kahrabaa'*	كهرباء
amber *kahramaan*	كهرمان
cave (n) *kahf, kuhoof*	كهف
hairdresser *kewafeer*	كوافير
glass (n, tumbler, etc.) *koob, akwaab*	كوب
elbow *koo', akwaa'*	كوع
tights *kolonaat*	كولونات
Kuwaiti *kuwaiteyy, kuwaitey-yeen*	كويتي
pillow case *kees wisaada*	كيس وسادة
how *kaif*	كيف
kilogram *keelograam*	كيلوجرام
kilometer *keelomitr*	كيلومتر
chemistry *keemyaa'*	كيمياء

ل (laam)

nobody *laa aHad*	لا أحد
nothing *laa shai'*	لا شىء
unbelievable *laa yuSad-daq*	لا يصدق
unbearable *laa yuTaaq*	لا يطاق
sign (n, display board) *laafita, laafitaat*	لافتة
pearl *lu'lu'a, lu'lu'*	لؤلؤة
because *la'ann*	لأن

lavender (n, plant) *lawanda*	لاونده
Lebanon *lubnaan*	لبنان
Lebanese *lubnaaneyy, lubnaaney-yeen*	لبناني
liter *litr*	لتر
moment *laHdha, laHdhaat*	لحظة
meat *laHm*	لحم
beef *laHm baqareyy*	لحم بقري
beard *liHya, liHaa*	لحية
tongue *lisaan, alsina*	لسان
thief (n) *liSS, luSooS*	لص
curse (n, evil spell) *la'na*	لعنة
language *lugha, lughaat*	لغة
why? *limaazha*	لماذا؟
ours *lina*	لنا
dialect; accent (n, speech) *lahja, lahjaat*	لهجة
if *lau*	لو
beans, runner *lubya*	لوبيا
lotus *lootos*	لوتس
keyboard (computer, etc.) *lawHat mafaateeH*	لوحة مفاتيح
almonds *lawz*	لوز
loofah *loofa*	لوفة
color (n) *lawn, alwaan*	لون
Libyan *leebeyy, leebey-yeen*	ليبي
Libya *leebya*	ليبيا
night *lail, layaali*	ليل
lime (citrus fruit) *laymoon akhDar*	ليمون أخضر
lemon *laymoon aSfar*	ليمون أصفر
lemonade *laymoonada*	ليمونادة

	م *(meem)*
except *maa 'adaa*	ما عدا
beyond *maa waraa'*	ما وراء
water (n) *maa'*	ماء
table (n) *maa'ida, mawaa'id*	مائدة
polite *mu'ad-dab*	مؤدب

what? *maadha*	ماذا؟
muezzin *mu'adh-dhin, mu'adh-dhineen*	مؤذن
minaret *mi'dhana, ma'aadhin*	مئذنة
March *maaris*	مارس
Maronite *maarooneyy, marooney-yeen*	ماروني
diamonds *maas*	ماس
past (adj) *maaDi*	ماض
temporary *mu'aq-qat*	مؤقت
money *maal*	مال
author (n) *mu'al-lif, mu'al-lifeen*	مؤلف
owner *maalik*	مالك
common (adj, familiar) *ma'loof*	مألوف
safe (adj, opp. risky) *ma'moon*	مأمون
mango *mango*	مانجو
exchange (n) *mubaadala*	مبادلة
match (n, sport) *mubaaraah*	مباراة
straight; direct (adj, non-stop) *mubaashir*	مباشر
wet (adj) *mubtall*	مبتل
early *mubak-kir*	مبكر
terminal (n, airport) *mabna al-maTaar*	مبنى المطار
late *muta'akh-khir*	متأخر
trouble (n) *mataa'ib*	متاعب
museum *matHaf, mataaHif*	متحف
translator; interpreter *mutarjim, mutarjimeen*	مترجم
undecided *mutarad-did*	متردد
even (adj, levelled) *mutasaawi*	متساو
volunteer (n) *mutaTaw-wi', mutaTaw-wi'een*	متطوع
advanced (adj) *mutaqad-dim*	متقدم
unstable *mutaqal-lib*	متقلب
contradictory *mutanaaqiD*	متناقض
mobile *mutanaq-qil*	متنقل
wild (adj, savage) *mutawaH-Hish*	متوحش
average; central; medium *mutawas-siT*	متوسط
available *mutawaf-fir*	متوفر
when? *matta*	متى؟
example *mithaal, amthila*	مثال
bladder *mathaana*	مثانة

cultured (erudite) *muthaq-qaf, muthaq-qafeen*	مثقف
like (similar to) *mithl*	مثل
triangle *muthal-lath, muthal-lathaat*	مثلث
risk (n) *mujaazafa, mujaazafaat*	مجازفة
complimentary; free (adj, gratis) *maj-jaaneyy*	مجاني
criminal (n) *mujrim, mujrimeen*	مجرم
magazine (periodical) *majal-la, majal-laat*	مجلة
frozen (adj) *mujam-mad*	مجمد
sum; total *majmoo'*	مجموع
group (n) *majmoo'a, majmoo'aat*	مجموعة
mad (crazy) *majnoon, majaaneen*	مجنون
unknown (adj) *majhool*	مجهول
accountant *muHaasib, muHaasibeen*	محاسب
lecture (n) *muHaadara, muHaadaraat*	محاضرة
attorney; lawyer *muHaami, moHaami-yeen*	محام
professional *muHtarif, muHtarifeen*	محترف
inevitable *maHtoom*	محتوم
engine *muHar-rik, muHar-rikaat*	محرك
station (n) *maHaT-Ta, maHaT-Taat*	محطة
lucky *maH-DHooDH*	محظوظ
store (n); shop (n) *maHal, maHal-laat*	محل
florist *maHall ward*	محل ورد
solution (n, liquid) *maHlool*	محلول
magnesium milk *maHlool al-magneezya*	محلول المجنيزيا
local *maHal-leyy*	محلي
ocean *muHeeT, muHeeTaat*	محيط
brain *mukh*	مخ
bakery *makhbaz, makhaabiz*	مخبز
crazy *makhbool*	مخبول
drug (narcotic) *mukhad-dir, mukhad-diraat*	مخدر
exit (n) *makhraj, makhaarij*	مخرج
beaten (adj, whisked) *makhfooq*	مخفوق
entrance *madkhal, madaakhil*	مدخل
coach (n, trainer) *mudar-rib, mudar-ribeen*	مدرب
amphitheatre *mudar-raj*	مدرج
school (n) *madrasa, madaaris*	مدرسة
heater *midfa'a*	مدفأة

urban (adj) *madaneyy*	مدني
director (n, senior executive) *mudeer*	مدير
city; town *madeena, mudun*	مدينة
flavor *madhaaq*	مذاق
masculine *mudhakkar*	مذكر
marvelous *mudh-hil*	مذهل
mirror *mir'aah, miraayaat*	مرآة
adolescent; teenager *muraahiq, muraahiqeen*	مراهق
square (n) *muraba', murab-ba'aat*	مربع
check (adj, pattern) *murab-ba'aat*	مربعات
jam (n) *murab-baa*	مربى
marmalade *murabba al-burtuqaal*	مربى البرتقال
once *mar-ra*	مرة
again (adv) *marra ukhra*	مرة أخرى
mattress *martaba, maraatib*	مرتبة
margarine *marjareen*	مرجرين
disease *maraD, amraaD*	مرض
diabetes *maraD as-suk-kar*	مرض السكر
refreshments *muraT-Tibaat*	مرطبات
boat *markib, maraakib*	مركب
central (adj, main) *markazeyy*	مركزي
exhausted *murhaq*	مرهق
fan (n, cooling) *marwaHa, maraawiH*	مروحة
traffic (n, cars, etc.) *muroor*	مرور
comfortable *mureeH*	مريح
ill; sick (person) *mareeD, marDaa*	مريض
auction (n) *mazaad, mazaadaat*	مزاد
double (adj) *muzdawaj*	مزدوج
farm (n) *mazra'a, mazaari'*	مزرعة
nuisance (adj) *muz'ij*	مزعج
chronic *muzmin*	مزمن
fake (adj) *muzayyaf*	مزيف
evening *masaa'*	مساء
help (n) *musaa'ida*	مساعدة
distance (n) *masaafa*	مسافة
equal (adj) *musawi*	مساو
responsible; in charge *mas'ool*	مسؤول

tenant (n) *musta'jir, musta'jireen*	مستأجر
impossible *mustaHeel*	مستحيل
round (adj, spherical) *mustadeer*	مستدير
orientalist *mustashriq, mustashriqeen*	مستشرق
hospital *mustashfa*	مستشفى
rectangle *mustaTeel, mustaTeelaat*	مستطيل
future (n) *mustaqbal*	مستقبل
independent *musta-qill*	مستقل
imported (adj) *mustawrad*	مستورد
level (n, water, etc.) *mustawa, mustawayaat*	مستوى
mosque *masjid, masaajid*	مسجد
powder (adj); powder (n) *masHooq, masaaHeeq*	مسحوق
theater (n, plays, etc.) *masraH, masaariH*	مسرح
play (n) *masraHey-ya, masraHey-yaat*	مسرحية
flat (adj, opp. bumpy) *musaT-TaH*	مسطح
mascara *maskaara*	مسكارا
sedative *musak-kin, musak-kinaat*	مسكن
obelisk *misal-la, misal-laat*	مسلة
elderly; old (person) *musinn, musin-neen*	مسن
Christian *maseeHeyy, maseeHey-yeen*	مسيحي
lattice window *mashrabeyya, mashrabey-yaat*	مشربية
drink (n) *mashroob, mashroobaat*	مشروب
liquor *mashroobaat rawHey-ya*	مشروبات روحية
busy (adj) *mash-ghool*	مشغول
problem *mushkila, mashaakil*	مشكلة
apricot *mishmish*	مشمش
famous; well-known *mash-hoor*	مشهور
expenses *maSaareef*	مصاريف
lamp *miSbaaH, maSaabeeH*	مصباح
Egypt *miSr*	مصر
Egyptian *misreyy, miSrey-yeen*	مصري
elevator *miS'ad, maSaa'id*	مصعد
factory *maSna', maSaani'*	مصنع
photographer *muSaw-wir, muSaw-wireen*	مصور
exact *maDbooT*	مضبوط
funny (humorous) *muD-Hik*	مضحك
stewardess *maDeefa, maDeefaat*	مضيفة

identical *muTaabiq*	مطابق
airport *maTaar, maTaaraat*	مطار
kitchen *maTbakh, maTaabikh*	مطبخ
press (n, printers, etc.) *maTba'a, maTaabi'*	مطبعة
rain (n) *maTar*	مطر
embroidered *moTar-raz*	مطرز
mallet *miTraqa khashabey-ya*	مطرقة خشبية
beaten (adj, frequented) *maTrooq*	مطروق
restaurant *maT'am, maTaa'im*	مطعم
antiseptic (adj) *muTah-hir*	مطهر
well done (cooking) *maT-hoo jay-yidan*	مطهو جيدا
envelope *maDHroof, maDHaareef*	مظروف
umbrella *miDHal-la, miDHal-laat*	مظلة
dark (unlit) *muDHlim*	مظلم
look (n, appearance) *maDHar, maDHaahir*	مظهر
with (prep) *ma'*	مع
down river *ma' majraa an-nahr*	مع مجرى النهر
together (adj) *ma'an*	معا
disabled (n) *mu'aaq*	معاق
landmarks *ma'aalim*	معالم
temple *ma'bad, ma'aabid*	معبد
moderate (adj) *mu'tadil*	متدل
infectious; contagious *mu'di*	معد
stomach (n) *ma'ida*	معدة
rate (n) *mu'ad-dal*	معدل
metal *ma'dan*	معدن
ferry (n) *mi'ad-dey-ya*	معدية
gallery; exhibition *ma'raD, ma'aariD*	معرض
exempt *ma'fi*	معفي
reasonable *ma'qool*	معقول
teacher *mu'al-lim, mu'al-limeen*	معلم
information *ma'loomaat*	معلومات
architect *mi'maareyy*	معماري
laboratory *ma'mal, ma'aamil*	معمل
meaning *ma'naa*	معنى
gastric; intestinal *ma'aweyy*	معوي
imperfect *ma'eeb*	معيب

adventure *mughaamara, mughaamaraat*	مغامرة
Moroccan *maghribeyy, maghaariba*	مغربي
ladle *maghrafa, maghaarif*	مغرفة
vain *maghroor*	مغرور
laundry (n, facility) *maghsala*	مفسلة
closed *mughlaq*	مغلق
unexpected (adj) *mufaaji'*	مفاجئ
surprise (n) *mufaaja'a, mufaaja'aat*	مفاجأة
key *muftaaH, mafaateeH*	مفتاح
open (adj) *maftooH*	مفتوح
mufti *mufti*	مفتي
missing *mafqood, mafqoodeen*	مفقود
useful *mufeed*	مفيد
tomb *maqbara, maqaabir*	مقبرة
knob (n, door handle, etc.) *miqbaD, maqaabiD*	مقبض
holy; sacred *muqad-das*	مقدس
down payment *muqad-dam*	مقدم
skimmed (adj, milk) *maqshood*	مقشود
imitation (adj, copied) *muqal-lad*	مقلد
brakes *makaabiH*	مكابح
treat (n); reward (n) *mukaafa'a*	مكافأة
call (n, a phonecall) *mukaalama, mukaalamaat*	مكالمة
place (n, location) *makaan, amaakin*	مكان
lodging *makaan iqaama*	مكان إقامة
Mecca *makka*	مكة
office *maktab, makaatib*	مكتب
post office *maktab al-bareed*	مكتب البريد
bureau de change *maktab Sar-raaf*	مكتب صراف
bookshop; library *maktaba, maktabaat*	مكتبة
macaroni *makarona*	مكرونة
nuts (n, walnuts, etc.) *mukas-saraat*	مكسرات
ingredients *mukaw-winaat*	مكونات
make-up (n, lipstick, etc.) *mikyaaj*	مكياج
sheet *milaa'a, milaa'aat*	ملاءة
clothes *malaabis*	ملابس
malaria *malarya*	ملاريا
sore *multahib*	ملتهب

salt (n) *malH, amlaaH*	ملح
spoon (n) *mil'aqa, malaa'iq*	ملعقة
king *malik, muluuk*	ملك
queen *malika, malikaat*	ملكة
laxative *mulay-yin, mulay-yinaat*	ملين
path *mamarr*	ممر
nurse *mumar-riDa, momar-riDaat*	ممرضة
boring (adj, tedious) *mumill*	ممل
kingdom *mamlaka, mamaalik*	مملكة
forbidden; prohibited *mamnoo'*	ممنوع
deadly; fatal; lethal *mumeet*	مميت
who? *man*	من؟
convenient; suitable; fitting *munaasib*	مناسب
occasion *munaasaba, munaasabaat*	مناسبة
dairy products *muntajaat al-albaan*	منتجات الألبان
resort (n) *muntaja', muntaja'aat*	منتجع
midnight *muntaSaf al-lail*	منتصف الليل
low *munkhafiD*	منخفض
representative (n) *mandoob, mandoobeen*	مندوب
salesman *mandoob mabee'aat*	مندوب مبيعات
handkerchief *mindeel*	منديل
towel *minshafa, manaashif*	منشفة
logic *manTiq*	منطق
landscape; scenery *manDHar, manaaDHir*	منظر
detergent *munaDH-DHif, munaDH-DHifaat*	منظف
charity (n) *munaDH-DHama khairey-ya*	منظمة خيرية
alone *munfarid*	منفرد
separately *munfaSileen*	منفصلين
engraved (adj) *manqoosh*	منقوش
skill (n) *mahaara, mahaaraat*	مهارة
filly *muhra*	مهرة
festival *mahrajaan*	مهرجان
important *muhimm*	مهم
engineer *muhandis, muhandiseen*	مهندس
reliable *mawthooq bih*	موثوق به
wave (n, in sea) *mawja, amwaaj*	موجة
banana *mawza, mawz*	موزة

razor *moos Hilaaqa*	موس حلاقة
music *museeqa*	موسيقى
fashion *moDa*	موضة
subject (n, topic) *mawDoo', mawDoo'aat*	موضوع
habitat *mawTin*	موطن
employee *muwaDH-DHaf, muwaDH-DHafeen*	موظف
appointment; date *maw'id, mawaa'eed*	موعد
stand (n, position) *mawqif, mawaaqif*	موقف
terminal (n, bus) *mawqaf al-otobees*	موقف الأوتوبيس
mummy *mumya'a, mumyawaat*	مومياء
mineral water *miyaah ma'daney-ya*	مياه معدنية
balance (n, scales) *meezaan*	ميزان
budget (n, fiscal framework) *meezaney-ya*	ميزانية
mechanic *mekaneeki*	ميكانيكي
harbor; port *meena', mawaani'*	ميناء

ن (noon)

asleep *naa'im*	نائم
lively *naabiD*	نابض
side (n) *naaHiya, nawaaHi*	ناحية
unusual; rare *naadir*	نادر
fire (n, flame) *naar*	نار
people *naas*	ناس
smooth (adj) *naa'im*	ناعم
fountain *nafoora, nafooraat*	نافورة
plant (n) *nabaat, nabaataat*	نبات
vegetarian *nabaateyy*	نباتي
wine *nabeedh*	نبيذ
result (n) *nateeja, nataa'ij*	نتيجة
carpenter *naj-jaar, naj-jaareen*	نجار
star (n) *nijm, nujoom*	نجم
brass *naHaas aSfar*	نحاس أصفر
misfortune (bad luck) *naHs*	نحس
bee *naHla, naHl*	نحلة
towards (prep) *naHwa*	نحو

thin *naHeef*	نحيف
marrow *nukhaa'*	نخاع
palm tree *nakhla, nakhl*	نخلة
eagle *nisr, nisoor*	نسر
textile *naseej*	نسيج
tapestry *naseej muzakhraf*	نسيج مزخرف
activity *nashaaT, anshiTa*	نشاط
energetic *nasheeT*	نشيط
crook *naS-Saab, naS-Saabeen*	نصاب
half *niSf, anSaaf*	نصف
advice (n) *naSeeHa, naSaa'iH*	نصيحة
optician *naDH-DHaraati*	نظاراتي
glasses *naDH-DHaara*	نظارة
system; order (n, method) *niDHaam, anDHima*	نظام
diet *niDHaam tagh-dheya*	نظام تغذية
clean (adj) *naDHeef*	نظيف
mint (n, herb) *ni'naa'*	نعناع
tunnel (n) *nafaq, anfaaq*	نفق
precious *nafees*	نفيس
stretcher *naq-qaala*	نقالة
point (n, dot) *nuqTa, nuqaTT*	نقطة
blood transfusion *naql dam*	نقل دم
pure *naqeyy*	نقي
final *nihaa'i*	نهائي
end (n) *nihaaya*	نهاية
seizure (n, fit) *nawba, nawbaat*	نوبة
Nubian *noobeyy, noobey-yeen*	نوبي
type (n) *naw', anwaa'*	نوع
raw *nayy'*	ني'

(haa) ه

quiet (adj) *haadi'*	هادئ
gift *hadey-ya, hadaaya*	هدية
this *haadha*	هذا
pyramid *haram, ahraam*	هرم

fragile *hash-sh*	هش
crescent *hilaal*	هلال
panic (n) *hala'*	هلع
here *huna*	هنا
there *Hunaak*	هناك
air (n) *hawaa'*	هواء
hobby *huwaaya, huwayaat*	هواية
hieroglyphic *heeroghleefee*	هيروغليفي

و (waaw)

sure *waathiq*	واثق
duty (n, obligation) *waajib, waajibaat*	واجب
oasis *waaHa, waaHaat*	واحة
valley *waadi, widyaan*	واد
loose (adj, baggy) *waasi'*	واسع
obvious; clear (adj, unambiguous) *waaDiH*	واضح
meal *wajba, wajbaat*	وجبة
face (n, anatomy) *wajh, wujooh*	وجه
destination *wijha, wijhaat*	وجهة
lonely *waHeed*	وحيد
amicable *wid-deyy*	ودي
hereditary *wiraathy*	وراثي
flower (n, rose, etc.) *warda, ward*	وردة
paper (n, sheet, etc.) *waraq, awraaq*	ورق
papyrus *waraq al-bardi*	ورق البردي
bay leaves *waraq al-ghaar*	ورق الغار
leaf *waraqat shajar, awraaq shajar*	ورقة شجر
lump; inflammation *waram, awraam*	ورم
vein (anatomy) *wareed, awrida*	وريد
weight (n) *wazn, awzaan*	وزن
middle *waSaT*	وسط
amid *wasT*	وسط
transportation *waseelat tanaq-qul*	وسيلة تنقل
handsome *waseem*	وسيم
recipe *waSfa, waSfaat*	وصفة

link waSla, waSlaat	وصلة
arrival wuSool	وصول
guardian waSeyy	وصي
vacancy (job opportunity) waDHaa'if khaaliya	وظائف خالية
job waDHeefa, waDHaa'if	وظيفة
promise (n) wa'd, wu'ood	وعد
loyal; faithful wafeyy	وفي
kneepad wiqaa' ar-rukba	وقاء الركبة
time (n, of day) waqt	وقت
fuel (n) waqood	وقود
agency (n) wikaala, wikaalaat	وكالة
birth (n) wilaada, wilaadaat	ولادة
United States al-wilaayaat al-muttaHida	الولايات المتحدة
boy walad, awlaad	ولد
unreal wahmeyy	وهمي

ي (yaa)

come (v) ya'tee	يأتي
hire (v); lease (v); rent (v) yu'aj-jir	يوجر
take ya'khudh	يأخذ
regret (v) ya'saf	يأسف
jasmine yasmeen	ياسمين
ruby (n) yaaqoot	ياقوت
confirm yu'ak-kid	يوكد
eat ya'kul	يأكل
hurt (v) yu'lim	يؤلم
order (v, demand) ya'mur	يأمر
hope (v) ya'mal	يأمل
exchange (v) yubaadil	يبادل
search (v) yabHath	يبحث
start (v); begin yabda'	يبدأ
remove yub'id	يبعد
stay (v); remain yabqa	يبقى
cry (v, weep) yabkee	يبكي
swallow (v, ingest) yabla'	يبلع

inform *yubal-ligh*	يبلغ
sell *yabee'*	يبيع
follow *yatba'*	يتبع
marinade (v); season (v, add spices) *yutab-bil*	يتبل
exceed *yatajaawaz*	يتجاوز
head (v, move towards) *yat-tajih*	يتجه
tour (v, visit extensively) *yatajaw-wal*	يتجول
move (v) *yataHar-rak*	يتحرك
train (v) *yatadar-rab*	يتدرب
remember *yatadhak-kar*	يتذكر
leave (v, abandon) *yatruk*	يترك
marry *yatazaw-waj*	يتزوج
climb (v) *yatasal-laq*	يتسلق
shop (v) *yatasaw-waq*	يتسوق
quarrel (v) *yatashaajar*	يتشاجر
call (v, phone someone) *yat-taS-Sil*	يتصل
imagine *yataSaw-war*	يتصور
tire (v) *yat'ab*	يتعب
trip (v, stumble) *yata'ath-thar*	يتعثر
learn (v) *yata'allam*	يتعلم
vomit (v) *yataqay-ya'*	يتقيأ
talk (v); speak *yatakal-lam*	يتكلم
expect *yatawaq-qa'*	يتوقع
trust (v) *yathiq*	يثق
pierce *yathqub*	يثقب
find (v) *yajid*	يجد
draw (v, attract) *yajdhub*	يجذب
tow (v); draw (v, pull behind) *yajurr*	يجر
sample (v, try) *yujar-rib*	يجرب
run (v, jog) *yajree*	يجري
sit *yajlis*	يجلس
try (v) *yuHaawil*	يحاول
love (v) *yuHibb*	يحب
like (v, enjoy) *yuHibb ann*	يحب أن
need (v) *yaHtaaj*	يحتاج
keep (v. retain) *yaHtafiDH*	يحتفظ
reserve; book (v) *yaHjiz*	يحجز

happen (v) *yaHduth*	يحدث
burn (v) *yaHriq*	يحرق
pack (v) *yaHzim*	يحزم
calculate *yaHsib*	يحسب
improve *yuHas-sin*	يحسن
obtain *yaHSul 'alaa*	يحصل على
inject (v) *yaHqin*	يحقن
resolve (a problem) *yaHill (mushkila)*	يحل (مشكلة)
shave (v) *yaHlaq*	يحلق
dream (v) *yaHlam*	يحلم
carry (v) *yaHmil*	يحمل
long (v, miss) *yaHinn*	يحن
turn (v, transform) *yuHaw-wil*	يحول
fear (v) *yakhaaf min*	يخاف من
tell *yukhbir*	يخبر
yacht *yakht, yukhoot*	يخت
select; choose *yakhtaar*	يختار
vanish *yakhtafee*	يختفي
direct (v, a movie, etc..) *yukhrij*	يخرج
deduct *yakhSim*	يخصم
vacate *yukhlee*	يخلي
hand (n, anatomy) *yad, ayaadi*	يد
save (v, set aside) *yad-dakhir*	يدخر
enter *yadkhol*	يدخل
smoke (v) *yudakh-khin*	يدخن
gossip (v) *yudardish*	يدردش
study (v) *yadrus*	يدرس
invite (v) *yad'oo*	يدعو
push (v); pay (v) *yadfa'*	يدفع
direct (v, give directions) *yadull*	يدل
manual (adj, by hand) *yadaweyy*	يدوي
run (v, operate) *yudeer*	يدير
owe *yadeen*	يدين
go *yadh-hab*	يذهب
melt; dissolve *yadhoob*	يذوب
watch (v, observe) *yuraaqib*	يراقب
win (v) *yarbaH*	يربح

tie (v) *yarbuT*	يربط
breed (v) *yurab-bi*	يربي
arrange *yurat-tib*	يرتب
rise (v) *yartafi'*	يرتفع
reply (v) *yarudd*	يرد
send *yursil*	يرسل
mail (v, letters) *yursil bil-bareed*	يرسل بالبريد
draw (v, illustrate) *yarsim*	يرسم
refuse (v) *yarfuD*	يرفض
raise (v) *yarfa'*	يرفع
dance (v) *yarquS*	يرقص
kneel *yarka'*	يركع
throw *yarmee*	يرمي
see *yara*	يرى
want (v) *yureed*	يريد
plant (v) *yazra'*	يزرع
increase (v) *yazeed*	يزيد
left (opp. right) *yasaar*	يسار
help (v) *yusaa'id*	يساعد
travel (v) *yusaafir*	يسافر
ask *yas'al*	يسأل
back (v, support) *yusaanid*	يساند
haggle (v) *yusaawim*	يساوم
swim (v) *yasbaH*	يسبح
relax *yastajim*	يستجم
use (v) *yastakhdim*	يستخدم
rest (v) *yastareeH*	يستريح
explore *yastakshif*	يستكشف
receive *yastalim*	يستلم
enjoy *yastamti'*	يستمتع
listen *yastami'*	يستمع
wake (v) *yastaiqiDH*	يستيقظ
pull (v) *yasHab*	يسحب
settle (v, pay) *yusad-did*	يسدد
hurry (v); rush (v) *yusri'*	يسرع
fall (v, tumble) *yasquT*	يسقط
live (v, dwell) *yaskun*	يسكن

allow; permit (v) *yasmaH*	يسمح
market (v) *yusaw-wiq*	يسوق
buy (v) *yashtaree*	يشتري
curse (v, abuse verbally) *yashtim*	يشتم
charge (v, fill up) *yash-Hin*	يشحن
drink (v) *yashrib*	يشرب
explain *yashraH*	يشرح
feel (v) *yash'ur*	يشعر
recover (from illness) *yushfa*	يشفى
complain *yashkoo*	يشكو
smell (v) *yashimm*	يشم
include *yashmal*	يشمل
construct *yushay-yid*	يشيد
point (v) *yusheer*	يشير
become *yuSbiH*	يصبح
dye (v) *yaSbigh*	يصبغ
believe *yuSad-diq*	يصدق
insist *yuSirr*	يصر
cry (v, yell) *yaSrukh*	يصرخ
catch (v, hunt successfully) *yaSTaad*	يصطاد
fish (v) *yaSTaaD samak*	يصطاد سمك
describe *yaSif*	يصف
park (v, cars, etc.) *yaSuff*	يصف
reach (v) *yaSil*	يصل
fix (v) *yuSliH*	يصلح
pray (v) *yuSal-lee*	يصلي
design (v) *yuSam-mim*	يصمم
make (v); manufacture *yaSna'*	يصنع
fast (v) *yaSoom*	يصوم
harass *yuDaayiq*	يضايق
set (v, clock, etc.) *yaDbuT*	يضبط
laugh (v) *yaD-Hak*	يضحك
beat (v, hit) *yaDrib*	يضرب
put *yadaa'*	يضع
join (v, connect) *yaDumm*	يضم
add *yuDeef*	يضيف
cook (v) *yaTbukh*	يطبخ

deport (v) *yaTrud*	يطرد
knock (v, on door, etc.) *yaTruq*	يطرق
feed (v) *yuT'im*	يطعم
extinguish *yuTfi'*	يطفئ
request (v) *yaTlub*	يطلب
dial (v) *yaTlub bit-tilifoon*	يطلب بالتليفون
launch (v, new product, etc.) *yuTliq*	يطلق
disinfect *yuTah-hir*	يطهر
fly (v) *yaTeer*	يطير
treat (v, behave towards) *yu'aamil*	يعامل
assist *yu'aawin*	يعاون
cross (v, movement) *ya'bur*	يعبر
apologize *ya'tadhir*	يعتذر
count (v, compute) *ya'id*	يعد
adjust *yu'ad-dil*	يعدل
limp (v) *ya'ruj*	يعرج
show (v); display; offer (v) *ya'riD*	يعرض
give *yu'Tee*	يعطي
know *ya'lam*	يعلم
teach *yu'al-lim*	يعلم
return (v) *ya'ood*	يعود
lend *yu'eer*	يعير
drown *yaghriq*	يغرق
wash (v) *yaghsil*	يغسل
cheat (v) *yaghish*	يغش
cover (v) *yughaTTi'*	يغطئ
package (v) *yughal-lif*	يغلف
boil (v, heat) *yaghlee*	يغلي
faint (v, pass out) *yughma 'alaih*	يغمى عليه
sing *yughan-nee*	يغني
change (v, money, etc.) *yughay-yir*	يغير
fire (v, terminate employment) *yafSil*	يفصل
prefer *yufaD-Dil*	يفضل
lose *yafqid*	يفقد
understand *yafham*	يفهم
fight (v) *yuqaatil*	يقاتل
accept *yaqbal*	يقبل

kill (v) *yaqtil*	يقتل
estimate (v) *yuqad-dir*	يقدر
read *yaqra'*	يقرأ
decide *yaqar-rir*	يقرر
divide (v) *yuqas-sim*	يقسم
cut (v, tear) *yaqTa'*	يقطع
vigilance *yaqDHa*	يقظة
stand (v, opp. sit); stop (v) *yaqif*	يقف
jump (v) *yaqfiz*	يقفز
shut (v); lock (v) *yaqfil*	يقفل
reduce *yuqal-lil*	يقلل
fry *yaqlee*	يقلي
say (v) *yaqool*	يقول
certainty *yaqeen*	يقين
write (v) *yaktub*	يكتب
repeat (v) *yukar-rir*	يكرر
hate (v) *yakrah*	يكره
break (v, smash) *yaksir*	يكسر
uncover *yakshif*	يكشف
complement (v, make whole) *yukam-mil*	يكمل
iron (v); press *yakwee*	يكوي
wear *yalbus*	يلبس
heal (mend) *yalta'im*	يلتئم
meet (v) *yaltaqee*	يلتقي
play (v) *yal'ab*	يلعب
turn (v, go around) *yalif*	يلف
spot (v, see) *yalmaH*	يلمح
touch (v) *yalmis*	يلمس
wave (v, with hand) *yulaw-wiH*	يلوح
compliment (v) *yamdaH*	يمدح
pass (v, go past) *yamurr*	يمر
tear (v, shred) *yumaz-ziq*	يمزق
wipe (v) *yamsaH*	يمسح
hold (v); catch (v) *yamsik*	يمسك
walk (v) *yamshee*	يمشي
fill (v) *yamla'*	يملأ
fill (v) *yamla'*	يملأ

have; own (v) *yamluk*	يملك
Yemeni *yamaneyy, yamaney-yeen*	يمني
right (opp. left) *yameen*	يمين
call (v, summon) *yunaadi*	ينادي
sleep (v) *yanaam*	ينام
wait (v) *yantaDHir*	ينتظر
succeed (v, opp. fail) *yanjaH*	ينجح
bleed *yanzif*	ينزف
slip (v, lose footing) *yanzaliq*	ينزلق
forget *yansa*	ينسى
join (v, enroll) *yanDamm*	ينضم
look (v, see) *yanzhur*	ينظر
organize (v) *yunaDH-DHim*	ينظم
refresh *yun'ish*	ينعش
burst (v) *yan-fajir*	ينفجر
save (v, rescue) *yunqidh*	ينقذ
grow *yanmoo*	ينمو
finish (v) *yunhee*	ينهي
intend (v) *yanwee*	ينوي
land (v) *yahbiT*	يهبط
quit *yahjur*	يهجر
cross (v, interbreed) *yahaj-jin*	يهجن
escape (v) *yahrab*	يهرب
mash (v) *yahris*	يهرس
Jew(ish) *yahoodeyy, yahood*	يهودي
agree *yuwaafiq*	يوافق
deposit (v, place securely) *yudi'*	يودع
connect *yawSil*	يوصل
deliver *yuwaS-Sil*	يوصل
sign (v, check, etc.) *yuwaq-qi'*	يوقع
day *yawm, ayaam*	يوم
daily *yawmeyy*	يومي

PHRASEBOOK CONTENTS

GETTING STARTED

Basics

If you travel in more than one Arabic speaking region, you will probably notice that simple words appear to vary from one place to the next. The Arabic words for "yes, hello, bread, why, now" will seem different, while the words for "political maneuvering" or "economic measures" will be the same – not that you will be discussing politics and economics in Arabic just yet. The phrases that follow should get you by. However, be prepared to hear variations in vocabulary and accent.

For "Please," either of the following expressions will do. Use whichever you find easier to pronounce.

Please.
من فضلك. / لو سمحت.
min faDlak/lau samaHt

Thanks.
شكرا.
shukran

Don't mention it.
عفوا.
afwan

yes
نعم
na'am

no
لا
laa

a little	large	open
قليل	كبير	مفتوح
qaleel	kabeer	*maftooH*
a lot	long	closed
كثير	طويل	مغلق
katheer	Taweel	*mughlaq*
some	short	black
بعض	قصير	أسود
ba'D	qaSeer	*aswad*
small	square	white
صغير	مربع	أبيض
Sagheer	murab-ba'	*abyaD*
medium	round	red
متوسط	مستدير	أحمر
muTawas-siT	mustadeer	*aHmar*

maybe
ربما
rub-bama

Sorry. My mistake.
آسف. غلطتي.
aasif. ghalTatee

Excuse me.
لا مؤاخذة.
lamu'akhdha

One moment.
لحظة.
laHza

Good idea.
فكرة عظيمة.
fikra 'aDHeema

why?
لماذا؟
limaadha

which?
أي؟
ayy

how?
كيف؟
kaif

When?

when?
متى؟
matta

before
قبل
qabl

after
بعد
ba'd

in the morning في الصباح *fiS-SabaaH*	today اليوم *al-yawm*
in the afternoon بعد الظهر *ba'd aDH-DHuhr*	yesterday أمس *ams*
in the evening في المساء *fil-masaa'*	tomorrow غدا *ghadan*

always
دائما
daa'iman

never
أبدا
abadan

sometimes
أحيانا
aHyaanan

a second	a day	a month
ثانية	يوم	شهر
thaneya	*yawm*	*shahr*
a minute	a week	a year
دقيقة	أسبوع	سنة
daqeeqa	*usboo'*	*sana*
an hour		
ساعة		
saa'a		

Where?

where?
أين؟
ain

Excuse me, where's the...?
لو سمحت، أين الـ...؟
law samaHt, ain al

here/there
هنا/هناك
huna/hunaak

right/left
يمين/يسار
yameen/yasaar

near/far
قريب/بعيد
qareeb/ba'eed

above/below
فوق/تحت
fawq/taHt

between
بين
bain

North/South
شمال/جنوب
shamaal/janoob

East/West
شرق/غرب
sharq/gharb

the Middle East
الشرق الأوسط
ash-sharq al-awsat

North Africa
شمال أفريقيا
shamaal afreeqia

the United States
الولايات المتحدة
al-wilaayaat al-muttaHida

Who?

who?
من؟
man

I/me	he/him	they/them
أنا	هو	هم
ana	*huwa*	*hum*
you (masc.)	she/her	you (pl.)
أنت	هي	أنتم
anta	*hiya*	*antum*
you (fem.)	we/us	
أنت	نحن	
anti	*naHnu*	

man
رجل
rajul

woman
إمرأة
imra'ah

child
طفل
Tifl

Greetings

As-salaamu alaikum is the classic, all-purpose phrase as one enters or leaves practically anywhere in the Arab World. Literally, it means "Peace is upon you." It is appreciated by most Arabic speakers, particularly Muslims, as it is also the official Islamic greeting. The official response is *wa 'alaikum as-salaam*. But if you want to dazzle, you can use the full-length version of the reply: *wa 'alaikum as-salaam wa-raHmat ulaahi wa barakaatuh* – which literally means "And peace is upon you too, as well as God's mercy and his blessings." The idea is that you are returning more than you have been offered.

Good morning.

صباح الخير.

SabaaH al-khair

Good evening.

مساء الخير.

masaa' al-khair

How are you?

كيف الحال

kaif al-Haal

Hello.

أهلا.

ahlan

Welcome.

مرحبا.

marHaban

Pleased to meet you.

فرصة سعيدة.

furSa sa'eeda

Congratulations!

مبروك!

mabrook

Many happy returns!

كل سنة وأنتم بخير!

kull sana wa-antum bi-khair

Happy Eid!

عيد سعيد!

'eed sa'eed

Bye!

مع السلامة!

ma'a s-salaama

Good night everyone!

تصبحوا على خير!

tiSbaHu 'ala khair

SETTLING IN AT THE RESORT/HOTEL

A wide variety of accommodation abounds in
the Middle East, from the modern, all-inclu-
sive beach resorts of the Red Sea, the Lower
Gulf, and the Mediterranean to small family-
run hotels and pensions in the towns.

In the resorts, almost everyone will speak
some English, especially at the front desk.
However, in the smaller establishments and
when dealing with more junior employees, a
few phrases of Arabic will be handy.

About the Room/Apartment

We'd like a room overlooking...

نريد غرفة تطل على...

nureed ghorfa tuTill 'ala

> the garden
>
> الحديقة
>
> *al-Hadeeqa*

> the sea
>
> البحر
>
> *al-baHr*

> the swimming pool
>
> حمام السباحة
>
> *Hammaam as-sibaaHa*

> the beach
>
> الشاطئ
>
> *ash-shaaTi'*

We'd like to add a...

نريد إضافة...

nureed iDaafat

> crib (cot)
>
> سرير أطفال
>
> *sareer aTfaal*

> bed
>
> سرير
>
> *sareer*

> pillow
>
> وسادة
>
> *wisaada*

> blanket
>
> بطانية
>
> *buTTaney-ya*

What time is...?

في أي ساعة...؟

fee ayy saa'a

> breakfast
>
> الإفطار
>
> *al-ifTaar*

> lunch
>
> الغداء
>
> *al-ghadaa'*

> dinner
>
> العشاء
>
> *al-'ashaa'*

Does this include...?

هل هذا يشمل...؟

hal haadha yashmal

    meals

    الوجبات

    al-wajbaat

    taxes

    الضرائب

    aD-Daraa'ib

    service

    الخدمة

    al-khidma

How do I turn this on?

كيف أشغل هذا؟

kaif ushagh-ghil haadha

How do I turn this off?

كيف أقفل هذا؟

kaif aqfil haadha

Do you have connecting rooms?

هل لديكم غرف متصلة؟

hal ladaikum ghuraf mut-taSila

Do you have a family room?

هل لديكم غرفة للعائلات؟

hal ladaikum ghurfa lil-'aa'ilaat

About the Bathroom/Kitchen

Show me how this works.

أريني كيف يعمل هذا.

areenee kaif ya'mal haadha

Can you fix this...?
ممكن تصلح هذا ...؟
mumkin tuSal-laH haadha

> flush
> السيفون
> *as-seefon*

> leak
> التنقيط
> *at-tanqeeT*

Where's this sound coming from?
من أين يأتي هذا الصوت؟
min ain ya'tee haadha S-Sawt

We'd like a few more of these.
نريد المزيد من هذا.
nureed al-mazeed min haadha

I think it's blocked.
أعتقد أنه مسدود.
a'ataqid annuh masdood

Send us some...
أرسلوا لنا بعض...
arseloo lana ba'ad

> insecticides
> المبيدات
> *al-mubeedaat*

> soap
> الصابون
> *aS-Saboon*

> towels
> المناشف
> *al-manaashef*

Sorry, we broke one of them.
آسف، كسرنا واحد منهم.
aasif, kasarna waaHid minhum

This gets too hot.
هذا يسخن جدا.
haadha yas-khan jid-dan

This doesn't get hot enough.
هذا لا يسخن كفاية.
haadha la yas-khan kifaaya

This gets too cold.
هذا يبرد جدا.
haadha yabrad jid-dan

This doesn't get cold enough.
لا يبرد كفاية
haadha la yabrad kifaaya

Will you take the trash away today?
هل ستأخذ الزبالة اليوم
hal sata'khuz az-zibaala al-yawm

Do you recycle...?
هل تعيدون دوران...
hal tu'eedoon dawaraan

   paper
   الورق
   al-waraq

   bottles
   الزجاجات
   az-zojajaat

   cans
   العلب
   al-'ilab

Please, clean...

من فضلك، نظف...

min fadlak, naZ-Zif

> beneath this
>
> أسفل هذا
>
> asfal haadha

> behind it
>
> وراءه
>
> waraa'uh

> above it
>
> فوقه
>
> fawquh

> inside it
>
> داخله
>
> daakhiluh

Keeping Yourself Occupied

Do you have ...?

هل عندكم...؟

hal 'andakum

> a sauna
>
> سونا
>
> sawna

> billiards
>
> بلياردو
>
> biliardo

> a gym
>
> جمنازيوم
>
> jimnaziom

daycare (a crêche)
حضانة
HaDaana

When is the belly dancer on?
متى موعد الراقصة؟
matta maw'id ar-raaqiSa

What time does the band start?
أي ساعة تبدأ الفرقة؟
ayy saa'a tabda' al-firqa

When does the folklore show finish?
متى ينتهي عرض الفنون الشعبية؟
matta yantahee 'arD al-funoon
ash-shaa'bey-ya

We need a baby sitter tonight.
نحتاج راعية للأطفال مساء اليوم.
naHtaaj raa'eya lil-aTfaal masaa' al-yawm

To get in, do I need to wear...?
للدخول، هل يجب أن أرتدي...؟
lid-dukh-ool, hal yajib an artadee

a tie
كرافتة
karafattah

a suit
بدلة
badla

proper shoes
حذاء لائق
hizaa' laa'iq

To get in, do I have to...?

للدخول، هل يجب أن...؟

lid-dukh-ool, hal yajib an

be over 18

أكون أكبر من ١٨

akoon akbar min tamantaashar

register

أسجل

usaj-jil

become a member

أشترك

ashtarik

buy a ticket

أشتري تذكرة

ashtaree tadhkara

ON THE MOVE

Getting from A to B

Traditionally, there wasn't a car-rental culture in Arabia similar to the one in the US or Europe. If you needed a car, a driver usually came with it. Things have changed in recent years, and a new car-rental culture has appeared, shaped by the standard international model of the industry. What this means is that once you step into a car rental company in Cairo or Dubai, for example, chances are the greeting, the discussion, and the forms will all be in English.

Public transport is different. On a local bus or train, you will probably need a few handy phrases.

car	airport	camel
سيارة	مطار	جمل
say-yaara	*maTaar*	*jamal*
bicycle	harbor	horse
دراجة	ميناء	حصان
dar-raaja	*meenaa'*	*HiSaan*
bus	station	walking
باص	محطة	المشي
baaS	*maHaT-Ta*	*al-mashyi*
train	ferry	ticket
قطار	معدية	تذكرة
qiTaar	*mi'ad-dey-ya*	*tadhkara*

How much is the ticket to...?
بكم التذكرة إلى ...؟
bikam at-tadhkara ila

How long is the trip?
كم تستغرق الرحلة؟
kam tastaghriq ar-riHla

Is there a delay?
هل هناك تأخير؟
hal hunaak ta'kheer

This luggage is...
هذه الأمتعة...
hadhihi l-amti'a

> heavy
> ثقيلة
> *thaqeela*

> light
> خفيفة
> *khafeefa*

> ours
> لنا
> *lana*

> not ours
> ليست لنا
> *laisat lana*

Is there air conditioning?
هل هناك تكييف هواء؟
hal henaak takyeef hawaa'

May we take this with us?
ممكن نأخذ هذا معنا؟
mumkin na'khudh haadha ma'ana

Excuse me, this is my seat.

لا مؤاخذة، هذا مقعدي.

laa mu'akhza, haadha miq'adee

Arranging a Cab

You are likely to use cabs during your stay. They are often more convenient and cheaper than renting a car. You will sometimes find larger cabs that seat several passengers. These ones follow a fixed route between destinations with the price shared between the passengers. Everyone has to wait until the cab is full before it leaves.

You can usually also hire a cab for the day, as well as for short trips. Tell the driver which places you want to visit and negotiate a rate in advance, which could include staying with you and bringing you back when you're finished. This may be easier than trying to pick up a different cab to get back later.

We need a cab for 4/5/6/7 passengers.

نحتاج تاكسي ٤/٥/٦/٧ ركاب.

naHtaaj taksi li-arba'/khamas/sitta/saba'a ruk-kaab

What's your whole-day rate?

ما أجرك للنهار كله؟

maa ajrak lin-nahaar kulluh

from ... in the morning

من ... صباحا

min ... Sabaahan

to ... in the afternoon

إلى ... بعد الظهر

ila ... ba'ad aDH-DHuhr

to ... in the evening

إلى ... مساء

ila ... masaa'an

Can you be here for us at ...?

ممكن تأتينا الساعة ...؟

mumkin ta'teena as-saa'a

How much to ...?

ما أجرك إلى ...؟

maa ajrak ila

then wait and bring us back tonight?

ثم تنتظرنا وترجعنا الليلة؟

thumma tantaDHirna wa-turaj-ji'na al-laila

then return to bring us back tomorrow?

ثم تعود لترجعنا غدا؟

thomma ta'ood li-turaj-ji'na ghadan

We're not in a hurry. Please slow down.

لسنا في عجلة. هدي السرعة من فضلك.

lasna fee 'ajala. had-di as-sur'a min faDlak

We're in a hurry. Can you go fast?

نحن في عجلة. ممكن تمشي بسرعة؟

naHnu fee 'ajala. mumkin tamshee bi-sur'a

If you must, stop and smoke outside.

أن كان لابد، قف ودخن في الخارج.

in kaan laabud, qif wa dakh-khin fil-khaarij

Could you shut the sun-roof?

ممكن تقفل فتحة السقف

mumkin taqfil fatHat as-saqf

Please take us to the ...

ممكن تأخذنا إلى ...

mumkin ta'khudhna ila

airport
المطار
al-maTaar

museum
المتحف
al-matHaf

harbor
الميناء
al-minaa'

city center
وسط البلد
wasT il-balad

Hopping on the Bus

You may choose to take a long-distance bus to go
from one town to the next, often an economical
way to travel. Try to avoid buses in large cities
during the rush hour – they can get extremely
crowded and hot.

Can we reserve seats?
ممكن نحجز مقاعد؟
mumkin naHjiz maqaa'id

Is there a discount for students?
هل هناك تخفيض للطلبة؟
hal hunaak takhfeeD liT-Talaba

Do we stop along the way?
هل سنتوقف في الطريق؟
hal sanatawaq-qaf fiT-Tareeq

Please, the radio is too loud!
من فضلك، الراديو عال جدا!
min faDlak, ar-radyo aalee jid-dan

May we open this window?

ممكن نفتح هذا الشباك؟

mumkin naftaH haadha sh-shub-baak

Are we getting nearer to the... ?

هل نحن نقترب من...؟

hal naHnu naqtarib min

>   terminal
>
>   المحطة
>
>   *al-maHaT-ta*

>   bridge
>
>   الجسر
>
>   *al-jisr*

>   tunnel
>
>   النفق
>
>   *an-nafaq*

>   river
>
>   النهر
>
>   *an-nahr*

When does the last bus leave?

متى يغادر آخر باص؟

matta yughaadir aakhir baaS

We'd like tickets for the first bus.

نريد تذاكر لأول باص.

nureed tadhaakir li'awwal baaS

Catching a Train

Trains can be romantic, and they don't get caught in traffic jams. The view out the window can be interesting, whether you are observing people going about their daily lives or simply admiring the desert scenery. Also you can doze off on a train, something you can't really do as a passenger in a car, nor indeed as the driver.

first class درجة أولى *daraja oola*	window seat بجوار الشباك *bi-jiwaar ash-shub-baak*
second class درجة ثانية *daraja thanya*	aisle seat على الممر *'alal mamar*
one way ذهاب *dhihaab*	sleeper عربة نوم *'arabat nawm*
round trip مع العودة *ma' al-'awda*	with bathroom مع حمام *ma'a Ham-maam*

Is there a smoking carriage?

هل هناك عربة للمدخنين؟

hal hunaak 'araba lil-mudakh-khineen

How do I get to platform number...?

كيف أصل إلى رصيف رقم...؟

kaif aSil ila raSeef raqm

Is it arriving on time?

هل يصل في موعده؟

hal yaSil fee maw'iduh

PLEASED TO MEET YOU

I'm From There

Generally, you will find people are friendly
and welcoming to foreign visitors. There are
those who are accustomed to seeing tourists
and have developed their own techniques of
selling them things. There are also those who
aren't used to seeing foreigners. They tend to
either stare, giggle, or both.

What's your name?

ما اسمك؟

maa ismak

How old are you

كم عمرك؟

kam 'umrak

I'm an American from...

أنا أمريكي من...

ana amreekeyy min

> Michigan
>
> ميتشيجان
>
> *mitshigaan*

> Seattle
>
> سياتل
>
> *siyaatil*

> California
>
> كاليفورنيا
>
> *kalifornya*

We're from...

نحن من...

naHnu min

> Canada
> كندا
> *kanada*

> Ireland
> ايرلندا
> *erlandaa*

> Australia
> استراليا
> *ostralyaa*

She's from...

هي من ...

hiya min

> Scotland
> اسكتلندا
> *iskutlanda*

> England
> انجلترا
> *ingiltera*

> New York City
> مدينة نيو يورك
> *madeenat nyoo york*

He's from...

هو من...

huwa min

New Zealand
نيو زيلندا
nyoo zeelanda

Florida
فلوريدا
Filoreeda

Washington State
ولاية واشنطن
wilaayat WashinTon

I'm originally from..., but I now live in...
أنا أصلي من.... لكن الآن أعيش في...
ana aSleyy min..., laakin al-ʌan a'eesh fee

My name is...
أنا اسمي...
ana ismee

I'm studying...
أنا أدرس...
ana adrus

anthropology *al-anthrobolojya* الانثروبولجيا
computing *al-kombyootir* الكومبيوتر
fashion *al-azyaa'* الأزياء،
history *at-taareekh* التاريخ
history of art *taareekh al-fenoon* تاريخ الفنون
law *al-qaanoon* القانون
music *al-mooseeqa* الموسيقى
nursing *at-tamreeD* التمريض
textiles *an-naseej* النسيج
languages *al-lughaat* اللغات

My family lives in... but I study in...

أسرتي تعيش في... ولكن أنا أدرس في ...

usratee ta'eesh fee ... wa laakin ana adrus fee

We're here...

نحن هنا...

naHnu huna

on a tour

في جولة

fee jawla

for business

في زيارة عمل

fee ziyaarat 'amal

doing research

للقيام ببحث

lil-qiyaam bi-baHth

on our honeymoon

في شهر العسل

fee shahr al-'asal

to check it out

لنستكشف الأمور

li-nastakshif al-umoor

for relaxation

للاستجمام

lil-istijmaam

Are you students?

هل أنتم طلبة

hal antum Talaba

I'm preparing my....

أنا أحضر...

ana uHaD-Dir

thesis

رسالتي

risaalatee

masters

الماجستير

al-majistair

PhD

الدكتوراه

ad-duktooraah

I am starting my new job next week.

سأبدأ وظيفتي الجديدة الأسبوع القادم:

*sa-abda' waDHeefatee al-jadeeda al usboo'
al-qaadim*

I'm currently unemployed, but I'm looking!

أنا حاليا بلا عمل، ولكني أبحث!

ana Haley-yan bilaa 'amal, wa laakin-nee abHath

I'm working on developing a...

أنا أعمل على انجاز...

ana a'mal 'ala injaaz

book idea

فكرة لكتاب

fikra li-kitaab

project

مشروع

mashroo'

business plan

خطة تجارية

khuT-Ta tujaarey-ya

Maybe I'll study Arabic in the fall.

ربما أدرس العربية في الخريف.

rub-bamaa adrus al-'arabey-ya fil-khareef

My Family & I

I've got kids back home.

أنا عندي أطفال في بلدي.

ana 'andi aTfaal fi baladee

Do you live with your parents?

هل تعيش مع أبويك

hal ta'eesh ma' abawaik

Your daughter looks just like you!

ابنتك تشبهك تماما!

ibnatik tashbihik tamaaman

Her mother seems quite young.

أمها تبدو صغيرة السن.

um-maha tabdoo Sagheerat as-sinn

Their daughter is very pretty.

ابنتهم جميلة جدا.

ibnathum jameela jid-dan

The older brother is so handsome.

الأخ الأكبر وسيم جدا.

al-akh al-akbar waseem jid-dan

Our youngest son wanted to come with us.

ابننا الأصغر كان يريد أن يأتي معنا.

ibnana al aSghar kaan yureed an ya'tee ma'na

His wife looks pregnant.

يبدو أن زوجته حامل.

yabdoo an zawjatuh Haamil

Small Talk

This is our first visit.

هذه أول زيارة لنا.

hadhihi aw-wal ziyaara lana

We are staying...

نحن نقيم...

naHnu nuqeem

> at the... hotel
>
> في فندق...
>
> *fi funduq*

> with our relatives
>
> مع أقاربنا
>
> *ma' aqaaribna*

> with friends
>
> مع أصدقاء
>
> *ma' aSdiqaa'*

We are visiting this place for...

نحن نزور هذا المكان لمدة..

naHnu nazoor haadha l-makaan li-mud-dat

> a week
>
> أسبوع
>
> *usboo'*

> two weeks
>
> أسبوعين
>
> *usboo'ain*

> a month
>
> شهر
>
> *shahr*

I'm here with my...

أنا هنا مع...

ana huna maa'

    (male/female) friend

    صديقي/صديقتي

    Sadeeqee/Sadeeqatee

    work colleagues

    زملائي في العمل

    zumalaa'ee fil-'amal

    father and mother

    أبي وأمي

    abee wi ummee

    grandfather and grandmother

    جدي وجدتي

    jid-dee wi jid-datee

    (male/female) roommate

    زميلي/زميلتي في الكلية

    zameelee/zameelatee fil-kuley-ya

What I like here most is the...

أكثر ما يعجبني هنا هو...

akthar maa yu'jibnee huna huwa

    weather

    الجو

    al-jaww

    food

    الأكل

    al-akl

    people

    الناس

    an-naas

I loved the...
أحببت ...
aHbabt

    market
    السوق
    as-sooq

    monuments
    الآثار
    al-aathaar

    flora
    النباتات
    an-nabaataat

I didn't like the...
لم تعجبني ...
lam tu'jibnee

    heat
    الحرارة
    al-Haraara

    traffic jams
    زحام المرور
    zaHaam al-moroor

    noise
    الضوضاء
    aD-DawDaa'

    dust
    الأتربة
    al-atriba

Next, we are planning to visit...
بعد هنا، ننوي زيارة...
ba'd huna, nanwee ziyaarat

WHERE TO TODAY?

Where is It?

Wandering around at your leisure, discovering a new place is fun. You could, however, end up slightly confused about where you are and how to get to where you want to be. These phrases will supplement your sense of direction.

In which direction should I head now?

في أي اتجاه أذهب الآن؟

fee ayy it-tijaah adh-hab al-aan

On the right or on the left?

على اليمين أم على اليسار؟

'alal yameen am 'alal yasaar

Will I find it....?

هل سأجده...؟

hal sa'ajid-duh

after the lights

بعد الإشارة

ba'd al-ishaara

before the bridge

قبل الجسر

qabl aj-jisr

above the shop

فوق المحل

fawq al-maHal

behind the mosque

وراء المسجد

waraa' al-masjid

facing the hospital

أمام المستشفى

amaam al-mustashfa

next to the cinema

بجوار السينما

bi-jiwaar as-sinema

between the florist and the bakery

بين محل الزهور والمخبز

bain maHall az-zuhoor wal-makhbaz

beneath that neon billboard

تحت هذا الإعلان المضئ

taHt haadha l-i'laan al-muDi'

in the center of the spice-merchants' market

في وسط سوق العطارين

fi wusT sooq al-'aT-Taareen

Holy Places. Old Towns.

Part of the attraction of cities like Cairo, Damascus, Marrakesh, or Baghdad must be walking through the ancient districts, alongside walls more than a thousand years old. It's exciting and humbling.

People still live in these quarters. So, maybe you'll hear the latest chart hits blasting through a lattice window, but don't let that distract you. Concentrate on the abundant charm and character. Enjoy the scent of history: a curious blend of spices, incense, and water-pipe tobacco.

Dress codes are really a question of judgement. For both men and women, they vary in strictness from country to country. But broadly speaking you don't want to stand out because of what you are wearing. Also, importantly, for women visiting a mosque or a church, avoid shorts and plunging necklines. A head-covering scarf is usually required. For men, this principle of judgement also applies. If it is unbearably hot, and you have to wear shorts, then make sure they are of a decent length.

We'd like to visit the...

نود زيارة...

nawad-du ziyaarat

> original city gates
> الأبواب الأصلية للمدينة
> al-abwaab al-aSleyya lil-madeena

> historical wall
> الحائط التاريخي
> al-Haa'iT at-taareekheyy

> ancient cemetary
> المدافن الأثرية
> al-madaafin al-atharey-ya

> old well
> البئر القديم
> al-bi'r al-qadeem

We intend to spend the morning at the...

ننوي قضاء الصباح في...

nanwee qaDaa' aS-SabaaH fee

> Ottoman Palace
> القصر العثماني
> al-qaSr al-'uthmaaneyy

> Islamic Museum
> المتحف الإسلامي
> al-matHaf al-islaameyy

Coptic Church
الكنيسة القبطية
al-kaneesa al-qibTey-ya

Jewish quarter
حي اليهود
Hayy al-yahood

What are the visiting hours in the...?
ما هي مواعيد الزيارة في...؟
maa hiya mawaa'eed az-ziyaara fee

mosque
المسجد
al-masjid

monastery
الدير
ad-dair

synagogue
المعبد اليهودي
al-ma'bad al-yahoodeyy

Please, where is the...?
لو سمحت، أين...؟
law samaHt, ain

museum
المتحف
al-matHaf

fortress
الحصن
al-HiSn

citadel
القلعة
al-qal'a

Please direct us to the...

من فضلك دلنا على الطريق إلى ...

min faDlak del-lena 'ala aT-Tareeq ila

> gold merchants
>
> تجار الذهب
>
> *tuj-jaar adh-dhahab*

> traditional silk market
>
> سوق الحرير التقليدي
>
> *sooq al-Hareer at-taqleedeyy*

> antiques' quarter
>
> حي تجارة الأنتيكات
>
> *Hayy tijaarat al-anteekaat*

Is photography allowed?

هل التصوير مسموح؟

hal at-tasweer masmooH

Can we see the actual grave?

هل يمكن أن نرى القبر نفسه؟

hal yumkin an nara al-qabr nafsuh

How did the calligrapher reach this ceiling?

كيف وصل الخطاط إلى هذا السقف؟

kaifa waSál al-khaTaaT ila haadha as-saqf

This must be a portrait of the caliph.

لابد أن تكون هذه صورة الخليفة.

laabud an takoon haadhihi Soorat al-khaleefa

Is it displayed inside the icon gallery ?

هل هي معروضة داخل قاعة الأيقونات؟

hal hiya ma'rooDa daakhil qaa'at al-aiqoonaat

Are they hanging outside the fresco exhibition?

هل هي معلقة خارج معرض لوحات الجبس؟

hal hiya mu'al-laqa khaarij ma'raD lawHaat aj-jibs

WHERE TO TODAY?

Holy Places. Very Old Towns.

Can you point the way towards the...

هل تدلنا على الطريق إلى...

hal tadul-lana 'ala aT-Tareeq ila

Valley of the Kings

وادي الملوك

waadi al-miluuk

Valley of the Queens

وادي الملكات

waadi al-malikaat

sphinx

أبو الهول

abu l-hawl

pyramids

الأهرامات

al-ahraamaat

temple

المعبد

al-ma'bad

old harbor

الميناء القديم

al-meenaa' al-qadeem

the abandoned pharaonic desert road

طريق الفراعنة الصحراوي المهجور

Tareeq al-faraa'ina aS-SaHraweyy al-mahjoo

Is it walking distance?

ممكن نمشيها؟

mumkin namshaaha

172   Arabic Dictionary & Phrasebook

o we have to cross the river?

هل يجب أن نعبر النهر

l yajib an na'bur an-nahr

abu Temple is on the West bank.

معبد هابو على البر الغربي

a'bad haaboo 'ala l-barr al-gharbeyy

it easy to find?

هل سأجدها بسهولة

l sa'ajidha bi-sohoola

an we fit them all into one excursion?

ممكن نزورها كلها في جولة واحدة

umkin nazooraha kul-laha fee jawla waaHida

the guide actually reading the hieroglyphics?

هل الدليل يقرأ الهيروغليفية

l ad-daleel yaqra' al-hiroghleefay-ya

the temple closed during the restoration work?

هل المعبد مغلق خلال أعمال الترميم

l al-ma'bad mughlaq khilaal a'maal at-tarmeem

vid colors	Thebes
ألوان زاهية	طيبة
waan zaahya	Teeba
lden mask	dynasty
قناع ذهبي	عهد الأسرة الحاكمة
naa' dhahabeyy	'ahd al-usra al-Haakima
und and light	papyrus
الصوت والضوء	ورق البردي
-Sawt waD-Daw'	waraq al-bardeyy

How long will the Abu Simbel trip take?

كم تستغرق رحلة أبو سمبل؟

kam tastaghriq riHlat abu simbel

Are you exhausted after that Karnak tour?

هل أنت مرهق بعد جولة الكرنك؟

hal anta murhaq ba'd jawlat al-karnak

We've had enough history for today.

أخذنا ما يكفينا من التاريخ اليوم.

akhadhna ma yakfeena min at-taareekh al-yawm

Now, I'd like to take the kids to the...

الآن، أود أن آخذ الأطفال إلى...

awadd an aakhudh al-aTfaal ila

> beach
> الشاطئ
> *ash-shaaTi'*

> playground
> ملاعب الأطفال
> *malaa'ib il-aTfaal*

> funfair
> حديقة الملاهي
> *hadeeqat il-malaahi*

LIFE IS A BEACH

The Blue Red Sea

All diving enthusiasts know about the Red Sea. Others should try snorkeling there at least once in their lives. The amazing colors down there have to be seen to be believed. And speaking of colors, the Red Sea is as blue as the next sea, if not bluer. It's just that the sandy hills along the coast have a reddish tint.

Compared to other seas, it is considered largely unspoilt.

Red Sea	Gulf of Suez
البحر الأحمر	خليج السويس
al-baHr al-aHmar	khaleej as-suwais
Mediterranean Sea	Indian Ocean
البحر الأبيض المتوسط	المحيط الهندي
al-baHr al-abyaD	al-muHeeT al-hindeyy
al-muTawas-siT	
Gulf of Aqaba	Atlantic Ocean
خليج العقبة	المحيط الأطلنطي
khaleej al-'aqaba	al-muHeeT al-aTlanTeyy

Is it safe to swim here?
هل السباحة هنا أمان
hal as-sibaaHa huna amaan

How do we contact the coastguard?
كيف نتصل بخفر السواحل
kaif nat-taS-Sil bi-khafar as-sawaaHil

sun	clouds
شمس	سحب
shams	*suHub*
moon	waves
قمر	أمواج
qamar	*amwaaj*
crescent	lake
هلال	بحيرة
hilaal	*buHaira*
full moon	river
بدر	نهر
badr	*nahr*
tide	fresh water
المد والجزر	مياه عذبة
al-madd wal-jazr	*miyaah 'azba*
temperature	salt water
درجة الحرارة	مياه مالحة
darajat al-Haraara	*miyaah maaliHa*
winds	waterfall
رياح	شلال
riyaaH	*shal-laal*
storm	oasis
عاصفة	واحة
'aaSifa	*waaHa*
humidity	water spring
رطوبة	عين
ruTuba	*'ain*
floods	sand dunes
سيول	كثبان الرمال
siyool	*kuthbaan ar-rimaal*

Gone Fishing

It's just as well there are no land-locked Arab countries, except perhaps for Iraq that only has a small outlet onto the Gulf. Arabian tourist destinations now realize that it is important to include water-based activities within the vacation packages they offer.

We'd like to rent some gear for…

نريد استئجار بعض أدوات…

nureed isti'jaar baa'D adawaat

> fishing
>
> صيد السمك
>
> *Said as-samak*

> diving
>
> الغطس
>
> *al-ghaTs*

> camping
>
> التخييم
>
> *at-takhyeem*

I am an experienced diver.

أنا غطاس ماهر.

ana ghaT-Taas maahir

He is a novice in fishing.

هو صياد سمك مبتدئ.

huwa Say-yaad samak mubtadi'

The mask leaks water.

نظارة البحر تدخل الماء.

nazaarat al-baHr tudkhil al-maa'

This is a suitable size wetsuit.

بدلة البحر مقاسها مناسب.

badlat al-baHr maqaasaha munaasib

The fins are too small for my feet.

الزعانف صغيرة جدا على قدمي.

az-za'aanif Sagheera jiddan 'ala qadamee

Can you arrange the...?

هل ممكن ترتب أنت...؟

hal mumkin turat-tib anta

> boat
>
> المركب
>
> *al-markib*

> bait
>
> الطعم
>
> *aT-Tu'm*

> ice
>
> الثلج
>
> *ath-thalj*

> drinks
>
> المشروبات
>
> *al-mashroobaat*

We will need to buy...

علينا أن نشتري...

'alaina an nashtaree

> sun glasses
>
> نظارات شمس
>
> *naDH-DHaaraat shams*

> a sun umbrella
>
> شمسية
>
> *shamsey-ya*

> sun screen
>
> كريم للشمس
>
> *kereem lish-shams*

I get sick on boats.

المراكب تصيبني بالدوار.

al maraakib tuSeebunee bid-dawaar

I used to be a swimming champion at school.

أنا كنت من أبطال السباحة في المدرسة.

ana kunt min abTaal as-sibaaHa fil-madrasa

The sea is rough today.

البحر هائج اليوم.

al baHr haa'ij al-yawm

Will we see the dolphins?

هل سنرى الدرافيل؟

hal sanara ad-daraafeel

The weather forecast for tomorrow is...

الجو غدا سيكون...

al-jaww ghadan sa-yakoon

> fair
>
> معتدل
>
> *mu'tadil*

> hot
>
> حار
>
> *Haarr*

> cold
>
> بارد
>
> *baarid*

How far is it from here roughly?

كم يبعد عن هنا تقريبا؟

kam yab'ud 'an huna taqreeban

Where is that place on the map?

أين هذا المكان على الخريطة؟

aina haadha l-makaan 'ala l-khareeTa

He appears to be an expert on...

يبدو أنه خبير في ...

yabdu annahu khabeer fi

> currents
>
> التيارات المائية
>
> *at-tayaaraat al-maa'ey-ya*
>
> corals
>
> المرجان
>
> *al-mirjaan*
>
> reefs
>
> الصخور
>
> *aS-Sukhoor*

Shall we set sail before sunrise?

هل نبحر قبل الشروق؟

hal nubHir qabl ash-shurooq

I prefer to return by sunset.

أفضل العودة وقت الغروب .

ufaD-Dil al-'awda waqt al-ghoroob

Look what the jelly fish has done to me.

انظروا ما فعل بي قنديل البحر .

unzuru ma fa'al bee qandeel al-baHr

Beach Party

A landscape dominated by desert makes water special. Any water is good, but fresh water is better.
This perhaps explains the affection we Arabs have
for water fountains. Traditionally, the sea has
offered us many rewards, like pearls, seafood, and
trade voyages to far away places. Today, many can
add tourism.

This is a wonderful place.

هذا المكان رائع.

haadha l-makaan raa'i'

Are these clothes appropriate?

هل هذه الملابس مناسبة؟

hal haadhihi l-malaabis munaasiba

Take my number and call me tomorrow.

خذ رقمي واتصل بي غدا.

khudh raqmee wa it-taSil bee ghadan

I will be here next Friday.

سأكون هنا يوم الجمعة القادم.

sa'akoon huna yawm al-jum'a al-qaadim

I would prefer it if we went together.

أفضل أن نذهب سويا.

ufaD-Dil an nadh-hab sawey-yan

Don't worry, I'll pay the bill.

لا تقلق، أنا سأدفع الحساب.

la taqlaq, ana sa'adfa' al-Hisaab

Let's take a walk on the beach.

هيا نتمشى على الشاطئ.

hay-ya natamash-sha 'ala sh-shaaTi'

Help me get this tar off my feet.

ساعدني في إزالة هذا القار عن قدمي.

saa'idni fi izaalit haadha al-qaar 'an qadami

I'm hungry. When do we eat?

أنا جعت. متى نأكل؟

ana ju't. mata na'kul?

I'll use this wood to light a fire.

أنا سأشعل النار بهذا الخشب.

ana sa-'ush'il an-naar bi-haadha l-khashab

Do you have a...
هل معك ...
hal ma'k

> match
> كبريت
> *kabreet*

> cigarette
> سيجارة
> *seegara*

> sweatshirt
> سويت شيرت
> *sweet shirt*

> can opener
> فتاحة علب
> *fat-taaHat 'ilab*

> condom
> عازل طبي
> *'aazil Tib-beyy*

> corkscrew
> فتاحة نبيذ
> *fat-taaHat nabeedh*

I don't enjoy taking risks.
أنا لا أحب المجازفة.
ana la uHibb al-mugaazafa

I don't feel comfortable about all this.
أنا لا أشعر بالراحة نحو كل هذا.
ana laa ash'ur bir-raaHa naHwa kull haadha

Keep your hands to yourself.
ابعد يديك عني.
ib'id yadaik 'annee

WHAT'S IN STORE

Advanced Shopping Techniques

Whether you are in a *sooq* or in an upmarket store, there will probably be something interesting urging you to buy and tempting you to spend. Remember not to look like you're too keen.

Haggling will probably be expected. You will probably enjoy it more if you treat it as lighthearted banter rather than as a battle of wills. Sellers will be pleased if you try speaking to them in Arabic. The whole exercise should be fun and have a happy ending.

My guess is that every tradesman you'll meet will know what the word "cash" means. You've got something to work with already.

How much is this?

بكم هذا؟

bikam haadha

Are you mad? That's too much!

هل أنت مجنون؟ هذا كثير جدا!

hal anta majnoon? haadha katheer jid-dan

You must be nuts! How much if I took...?

أنت أكيد مخبول! بكم لو أخذت...؟

anta akeed makhbool! bikam law akhadht

two

اثنين

ithnain

four
أربعة
arba'a

the whole box
الصندوق كله
aS-Sandooq kul-luh

Is this the...?
هل هذا...؟
hal haadha

final price
آخر سعر
aakhir si'r

cash price
سعر الكاش
s'ir ak-kaash

Is this the price per...?
هل هذا سعر...؟
hal haadha si'r

meter
المتر
al-mitr

kilo
الكيلو
ak-kilo

centiliter
السنتيلتر
as-santilitr

gram
الجرام
aj-jiraam

I'd like to see a selection of...

أريد أن أرى تشكيلة من...

ureed an ara tashkeela min

> sizes
> الأحجام
> *al-aHjaam*

> colors
> الألوان
> *al-alwaan*

> shapes
> الأشكال
> *al-ashkaal*

> styles
> الموديلات
> *al-mudeel-laat*

Will you be giving us a...?

هل ستعطينا...؟

hal satu'Teena

> receipt
> إيصال
> *eeSaal*

> guarantee
> ضمان
> *Damaan*

> instructions booklet
> كتيب الإرشادات
> *kutayyib al-irshadaat*

> certificate
> شهادة
> *shihaada*

You have to give us...
يجب أن تعطينا...
yajib an tu'Teena

    a discount
    تخفيض
    takhfeeD

    a free one
    واحدة مجانا
    waHida maj-jaanan

    the other at half price
    الأخرى بنصف السعر
    al-ukhra bi-niSf as-si'r

It's a deal.
اتفقنا.
it-tafaqna

Forget about it.
يفتح الله.
yiftaH allah

Shopping For Others

I need a gift that is suitable...
أريد هدية مناسبة...
ureed hadeyya munaasiba

    for my wife
    لزوجتي
    li-zawjatee

    for my husband
    لزوجي
    li-zawjee

    for my son
    لابني
    l-ibnee

for my daughter
لإبنتي
l-ibnatee

for my father
لأبي
li-'abee

for my mother
لأمي
li-ummee

for my (male) friend
لصديقي
li-SaDeeqee

for my (female) friend
لصديقتي
li-SaDeeqatee

I need to buy a souvenir costing around...
أريد شراء، تذكار سعره في حدود...
ureed shiraa' tizkaar, si'ruh fee Hudood

His hobbies are...
هواياته هي...
huwaayaatuh hiya

photography
التصوير
at-taSweer

carpentry
النجارة
an-nijaara

sports
الرياضة
ar-riyaaDa

She loves...

إنها تحب...

in-naha tuHibb

> painting
>
> الرسم
>
> *ar-rasm*

> music
>
> الموسيقى
>
> *al-museeqa*

> embroidery
>
> التطريز
>
> *at-taTreez*

They are both keen on...

الاثنان يحبان...

al-ithnaan yuHib-baan

> equestrian pursuits
>
> الفروسية
>
> *al-furusey-ya*

> desert hikes
>
> التجول في الصحراء
>
> *at-tajaw-wul fis-saHraa'*

> camping
>
> التخييم
>
> *at-takhyeem*

Do you have something for antique collectors?

هل عندك شئ؛ لهواة جمع التحف القديمة؟

hal 'andak shai' li-huwaah jam'at-tuHaf al-qadeema

I would prefer the colors to be...

أنا أفضل أن تكون الألوان...

ana ufaD-Dil an takoon al-alwaan

darker

أغمق

aghmaq

lighter

أفتح

aftaH

This scent does not suit my skin.

هذا العطر لا يناسب جلدي.

haadha l-i'Tr la yunaasib jildee

I know it is an imitation.

أنا أعرف أنه مقلد.

ana a'rif annuh muqal-lad

If I buy the saddle, do you arrange shipping?

لو اشتريت السرج، هل ترتبون الشحن؟

law ishtarait as-sarj, hal turat-tiboon ash-shaHn

We'll be back after touring the commercial district

سنعود بعد جولتنا في الحي التجاري.

sana'uud ba'd jawlatna fil-Hayy at-tijaareyy

I Need It. What Is It?

What do they sell in this shop?

ماذا يبيعون في هذا المحل؟

maadha yabee'oon fee haadha l-maHall

What's this man making?

ماذا يصنع هذا الرجل؟

maadha yaSna' haadha r-rajul

Is this...?

هل هذا...؟

hal haadha

  copper

  نحاس أحمر

  naHaas aHmar

  brass

  نحاس أصفر

  naHaas aSfar

  silver

  فضة

  fiDDah

  gold

  ذهب

  dhahab

  gold plated

  ذهب قشرة

  dhahab qishra

  hand made

  شغل يد

  shughl yad

  leather

  جلد

  jild

  wood

  خشب

  khashab

  ivory

  عاج

  'aaj

It's a familiar scent. Is it the essence of...?

عطره مألوف. هل هو خلاصة...؟

'iTruh ma'loof. hal huwa khulaaSat

> jasmine
> الياسمين
> *al-yaasmeen*

> narcissus
> النرجس
> *an-narjis*

> musk
> المسك
> *al-misk*

> ambergris
> العنبر
> *al-'anbar*

> lavender
> اللاونده
> *al-laawanda*

> Arabian Jasmine
> الفل
> *al-full*

I will take the engraved one.

سآخذ المنقوش.

sa'aakhudh al-manqoosh

What's this stone?

ما هذا الحجر؟

ma haadha l-hajar

> amber
> كهرمان
> *kahramaan*

carnelian

عقيق أحمر

'aqeeq aHmar

emerald

زمرد

zumur-rud

ruby

ياقوت أحمر

yaaqoot aHmar

green corundum

ياقوت أخضر

yaaqoot akhDar

diamond

ماس

maas

twenty-four carat

أربعة وعشرين قيراط

arba'a wa 'ishreen qeeraaT

Is this area famous for pottery?

هل هذه المنطقة مشهورة بالفخار؟

hal haadhihi l-mantiqa mash-hoora bil-fukh-khaar

What kind of material is this?

ما هو نوع هذا القماش؟

maa huwa naw' haadha l-qumaash

I wonder if it's the right measurement.

هل المقاس مضبوط يا ترى.

hal al-maqaas maDbooT yaa tura

I know exactly where I will put this carpet.

أنا أعرف بالتحديد أين سأضع هذه السجادة.

ana a'raf bit-taHdeed aina sa'Da' hadhihi s-sij-jaada

What's the difference between … carpets?

ما هو الفرق بين السجاد…؟

ma huwa l-farq bain as-sijaad

> Asfahani
>
> أصفهاني
>
> *aSfahaaneyy*

> Kermani
>
> كرماني
>
> *kirmaaneyy*

> Shiraazi
>
> شيرازي
>
> *sheeraazeyy*

Please teach me how to…

من فضلك علمني كيف…

min fadlak 'allimnee kaif

> use it
>
> أستعمله
>
> *asta'miluh*

> assemble it
>
> أركبه
>
> *urak-kibbuh*

> prepare it
>
> أحضره
>
> *uhaD-Diruh*

> mix it
>
> أخلطه
>
> *akhliTuh*

LET'S EAT

Tastes Familiar!

The good thing about this list of food items is that the Arabic names are close to the English and therefore should sound familiar to you. Now you know that at least you won't starve.

tuna تونة *toona*

pizza بيتزا *beetza*

burger بورجر *boorgar*

macaroni مكرونة *makarona*

ice-cream آيس-كريم *aayis-kreem*

toast توست *tost*

lemon ليمون *laimoon*

cake كيك *kaik*

spaghetti اسباجيتي *isbaaget-ti*

roast beef روزبيف *rozbeef*

salad سلطة *salaTa*

grapefruit جريب فروت *gireib firoot*

hummus حمص *Hum-muS*

tomato طماطم *TamaaTim*

fillet فيليه *feeleih*

tamarind تمر هندي *tamr hindi*

carob خروب *khar-roob*

mustard مسطردة *musTarda*

biscuit بسكوت *baskoot*

omlette اومليت *omleet*

cream كريمة *kreema*

steak استيك *isteek*

spinach سبانخ *sabaanikh*

sardines سردين *sardeen*

mango مانجو *mango*

beer بيرة *beera*

cumin كمون *kam-mooon*

guava جوافة *gawaafa*

potato chips بطاطس شيبس *baTaaTis shibs*

chocolate شوكولاتة *shokolaata*

But here is a list that won't sound familiar at all.

honey عسل 'asal
rice رز ruzz
cheese جبنة jubna
pigeon حمام Hamaam
bread خبز khubz
zuccini كوسة koosa
eggplant باذنجان baadhinjaan
apricot مشمش mish-mish
olives زيتون zaitoon
dates بلح balaH
sugar cane قصب qaSab
vine leaves ورق عنب waraq 'inab
butter زبد zubd
rabbit أرانب araanib
carrot جزر jazar
figs تين teen
duck بط baTT
banana موز mawz
ghee سمن samn
cucumber خيار khiyaar
garlic ثوم thawm
salt ملح malH
pepper فلفل filfil
parsley بقدونس baqdoonis

With a Pinch

"Did I eat the same thing in Turkey? I thought this was a Greek dish! That's exactly what we had in Syria! Is this the Egyptian way of cooking it, or is it the Lebanese?" Actually, the origins are probably a mish-mash of the recipes that blended as they travelled through the eastern Mediterranean without restrictions. Now, with such an incestuous background, every cuisine tends to think their own is the original and the best. If you are cornered and are asked to take sides, wear your best smile, nod tactfully, and continue to munch away.

Does it contain...?

هل يحتوي على...؟

hal yaHtawi 'ala

nuts

مكسرات

mukas-saraat

meat

لحم

laHm

sugar

سكر

suk-kar

I'm not allowed...

ممنوع عني...

mamnoo' 'anni

fish

السمك

as-samak

eggs

البيض

al-baiD

strawberries

الفراولة

al-farawla

milk

الحليب

al-Haleeb

alcohol

الكحول

al-kuHool

broiled	charcoal-grilled
مشوي	على الفحم
mashweyy	*'ala l-faHm*
fried	with
مقلي	مع
maqleyy	*ma'*
stuffed	without
محشي	بدون
maHsheyy	*bidoon*
mashed	a lot
مهروس	كثير
mahroos	*katheer*
grated	a little
مبشور	قليل
mabshoor	*qaleel*
sliced	dish of the day
شرائح	طبق اليوم
sharaa'iH	*Tabaq al-yawm*
ground	vegetarian
مفروم	نباتي
mafroom	*nabaateyy*
oven-baked	low-fat
في الفرن	دون دهون
fil-furn	*doon dihoon*
steamed	without chili
على البخار	دون شطة
'ala l-bukhaar	*doon shaT-Ta*

I must try this!

يجب أن أذوق هذا!

yajib an adhooq haadha

This looks yummy.

هذا شكله لذيذ.

haadha shakluh ladheedh

The other dish smells better.

الطبق الآخر رائحته أطيب.

aT-Tabaq al-aakhar raa'iHatuh aTyab

May we try this?

ممكن نجرب هذا؟

mumkin nujar-rib haadha

I want the recipe now.

أريد الوصفة الآن.

ureed al-waSfa al-aan

Table Four

We will wait for a table that's...

سننتظر مائدة تكون...

sanantaDHir maa'ida takoon

> bigger
>
> أكبر
>
> *akbar*

> outside
>
> في الخارج
>
> *fil-khaarij*

> by the sea
>
> على البحر
>
> *'ala l-baHr*

> in the shade
>
> في الظل
>
> *fiDH-DHill*

We want to try a local dish.

نريد أن نجرب أكلة محلية.

nureed an nujar-rib akla maHal-ley-ya

Maybe we'll start with a selection of appetizers.

ربما بدأنا بتشكيلة من المقبلات.

rub-bama bada'na bi-tashkeela min al-muqbilaat

A bottle of mineral water, please.

زجاجة مياه معدنية، من فضلك.

zujaajat miyaah ma'daney-ya, min faDlak

Egyptian مصري *miSreyy*	French فرنسي *faranseyy*
Lebanese لبناني *lubnaaneyy*	Indian هندي *hindeyy*
Moroccan مغربي *mahgribeyy*	Spanish أسباني *asbaaneyy*
Italian ايطالي *eeTaaleyy*	Thai تايلاندي *tailandeyy*
Chinese صيني *Seeneyy*	Japanese ياباني *yabaaneyy*
Greek يوناني *yunaaneyy*	Iranian إيراني *eeraaneyy*

Can you give us...?

ممكن تعطينا...؟

mumkin tu'Teena

a fork

شوكة

shooka

a knife

سكين

sik-keen

a spoon

ملعقة

mil'aqa

salt

ملح

malH

pepper

فلفل

filfil

oil

زيت

zait

vinegar

خل

khall

no milk/sugar

دون حليب/سكر

doon Haleeb/suk-kar

with ice

مع ثلج

ma' thalj

The food is...

الأكل...؟

al-akl

> warm
>
> ساخن
>
> *saakhin*
>
> cold
>
> بارد
>
> *baarid*
>
> frozen
>
> مجمد
>
> *mujam-mad*

I never thought one day I'd eat...

لم يخطر لي أني سآكل يوما...

lam yakhTur lee annee saakul yawman

> goat meat
>
> لحم الماعز
>
> *laHm al-maa'iz*
>
> raw liver
>
> كبة نية
>
> *kib-ba nayya*
>
> sheep's testicles
>
> مخاصي
>
> *makhaaSee*

Are the coffee beans ground with cardamom?

هل البن مطحون مع حب الهال؟

hal al-bunn maT-Hoon ma' Habb al-haal

The check please.

الحساب من فضلك.

al-Hisaab min faDlak

DOWN TO BUSINESS

My Line of Work

I'm a...
أنا...
ana

> (male/female) lawyer
> محام/محامية
> *muHaami/muHaamiya*

> (male/female) nurse
> ممرض/ممرضة
> *mumar-riD/mumar-riDa*

> (male/female) engineer
> مهندس/مهندسة
> *muhandis/muhandisa*

> (male/female) designer
> مصمم/مصممة
> *muSam-mim/muSam-mima*

> (male/female) accountant
> محاسب/محاسبة
> *muHaasib/muHaasiba*

> (male/female) teacher
> مدرس/مدرسة
> *mudarris/mudarrisa*

I work in a...
أنا أعمل في...
ana a'mal fee

oil field

حقل بترول

Haql bitrool

satellite TV station

محطة فضائية

maHaT-Ta faDaa'ey-ya

shop

محل

maHall

hair salon

كوافير

kuwaafeer

children's nursery

دار حضانة

daar HaDaana

ad agency

وكالة إعلان

wikaalat i'laan

I work in the field of...

أنا أعمل في مجال...

ana a'mal fee majaal

marketing

التسويق

at-tasweeq

distribution

التوزيع

at-tawzee'

human resources

شؤون العاملين

shu'oon al-'aamileen

I specialize in...

مجال تخصصي هو...

majaal takhaS-SoSi huwa

> sales
>
> المبيعات
>
> *al mabee'aat*

> computers
>
> الكومبيوتر
>
> *al-kombyootir*

> publishing
>
> النشر
>
> *an-nashr*

> export
>
> التصدير
>
> *at-taSdeer*

> import
>
> الإستيراد
>
> *al-isteeraad*

> manufacturing
>
> التصنيع
>
> *at-taSnee'*

I buy and sell...

أنا أشتري وأبيع...

ana ashtaree wa abee'

> shares
>
> الأسهم
>
> *al-as-hum*

> real estate
>
> العقارات
>
> *al-'aqaaraat*

My job is with...

وظيفتي هي مع ...

wazeefatee hiya ma'

> the government
>
> الحكومة
>
> *al-Hukooma*

> our embassy here
>
> سفارتنا هنا
>
> *sifaaratna huna*

> a charity
>
> منظمة خيرية
>
> *munaDH-DHama khay-rey-ya*

I am a consultant in...

أنا مستشار في ...

ana mustashaar fee

> finance
>
> التمويل
>
> *at-tamweel*

> investments
>
> الاستثمارات
>
> *al-istithmaaraat*

> legal affairs
>
> الشؤون القانونية
>
> *ash-shu'oon al-qaanooney-ya*

I assist my husband in running the business.

أنا أعاون زوجي في إدارة العمل .

ana 'u'aawin zawjee fee idarat al-'amal

I work from home.

أنا أعمل في البيت .

ana a'mal fil-bait

I'm a journalist. My job's to ask.

أنا صحافية. أسئلتي هي عملي.

ana SaHaafey-ya. as'ilatee hiya 'amalee

Compu-speak @ Work

Our IT manager has the answers.

مدير أنظمة المعلومات لديه الإجابات.

mudeer anDHimat al-ma'loomaat ladaihi al-ijaabaat

solutions	digital
حلول	رقمي
Hulool	*raqmeyy*
high speed	database
عالية السرعة	قاعدة بيانات
'aleyat as-sur'a	*qaa'idat bayaanaat*
scanner	applications
آلة مسح	تطبيقات
aalat masH	*taTbeeqaat*
operating system	communications
نظام تشغيل	اتصالات
niDHaam tash-gheel	*it-tiSaalaat*
search engine	disc
آلة بحث	قرص
aalat baHth	*qurS*
color copier	peripheral
ناسخة ملونة	طرفي
naasikha mulaw-wana	*tarafeyy*
printer	upgrade
طابعة	ترقية
Taabi'a	*tarqey-ya*

We have plenty of time.

عندنا وقت كثير

'indana waqt katheer

The accountant usually deals with these issues.

المحاسب يتولى هذه الأمور عادة.

al-muHaasib yatawal-la haadhihi l-umoor 'aadatan

We can solve this problem next week.

يمكننا أن نحل هذه المشكلة الأسبوع القادم.

yumkin-na an naHil haadhihi al-mushkila
al-usboo' al-qaadim

Do you speak any other languages?

هل تتكلم لغات أخرى؟

hal tatakal-lam lughaat ukhra

Do you understand what I'm saying?

هل تفهم ما أقول؟

hal tafhamoon ma aquul

Sorry, I don't understand what you mean.

آسف، أنا لا أفهم ما تقصده.

aasif, ana la afham ma taqSuduh

When is the day off?

متى يوم الإجازة؟

matta yawm al-ijaaza

Is it closed during prayer times?

هل يقفل في أوقات الصلاة؟

hal yaqfil fee awqaat aS-Salaah

What will be the Ramadan hours?

ماذا ستكون مواعيد رمضان؟

maadha satakuun mawaa'eed ramaDaan

closed Friday	before the feast
مغلق الجمعة	قبل العيد
mughlaq aj-jum'a	*qabl al-'eed*
open Sunday	in the lunch break
مفتوح الأحد	في فترة الغداء
maftooH al-aHad	*fee fatrat al-ghadaa'*
half-day Thursday	after prayers
الخميس نصف يوم	بعد الصلاة
al-khamees niSf yawm	*ba'd aS-Salaah*

Send It Home

Is this the right window for...?
هل هذا هو شباك...؟
hal haadha huwa shub-baak

air mail
البريد الجوي
al-bareed al-jaw-weyy

registered
مسجل
musaj-jal

regular
عادٍ
'aadi

These postcards and the necessary stamps to...
هذه البطاقات مع الطوابع اللازمة إلى...
hadhihi l-biTaaqaat ma' aT-Tawaabi' al-laazima ila

Your colleague over there sent me to you.
زميلك الذي هناك أرسلني لك.
zameelak aladhee hunaak arsalanee lak

Do I fill these forms now?

هل أملأ هذه الاستمارات الآن؟

hal amla' haadhihi l-istimaaraat al-aan

Do you know when it gets there?

هل تعرف متى تصل إلى هناك؟

hal ta'rif matta taSil ila hunaak

Do you need my passport for anything?

هل تحتاج لجواز سفري في شيء؟

hal taHtaaj li-jawaaz safaree fee shai'

Will I need insurance against damage?

هل سأحتاج إلى التأمين ضد التلف؟

hal sa-aHtaaj ila t-ta'meen Didd at-talaf

letter	address
خطاب	عنوان
khiTaab	*'unwaan*
envelope	name
مظروف	الاسم
maDHroof	*al-ism*
stamp	date of birth
طابع بريد	تاريخ الميلاد
Taabi' bareed	*taareekh al-meelaad*
weight	occupation
وزن	المهنة
wazn	*al-mihna*
value	
قيمة	
qeema	

I will change some money and be right back.

سأغير بعض النقود وأرجع حالا .

sa-ughay-yir ba'd an-nuqood wa-arja' Haalan

I will give you the details of my account.

سأعطيك تفاصيل حسابي .

sa-u'Teek tafaaSeel Hisaabee

In which box please?

في أي صندوق من فضلك؟

fee ayy Sandooq min faDlak

I understand all you say, except the word....

فهمت كل ما تقول، ماعدا كلمة...

fahimt kull maa taqool, ma 'ada kalimat

WHEN THE GOING GETS TOUGH

Health and Well-being

Thankfully, I have not yet met a doctor who cannot understand basic medical English. The syllabus at medical school is taught in English. But speaking to the person you meet before you get to the doctor, such as a junior nurse whose grasp of English may not be all that good, could be tricky.

Do we take him to the hospital now?

هل نأخذه إلى المستشفى الآن؟

hal na'khudhuh ila al-mustashfa al-aan

I am pregnant in my... month.

أنا حامل في الشهر...

ana Haamil fish-shahr...

Tell the nurse that my friend is...

قل للمرضة أن صديقي...

qul lil-mumar-riDa an Sadeeqee

> pale
>
> شاحب
>
> *shaaHib*
>
> having a seizure
>
> مصاب بالنوبة
>
> *muSaab bin-nawba*
>
> has a rash
>
> عنده طفح جلدي
>
> *'anduh TafH jildeyy*
>
> vomiting
>
> يتقيأ
>
> *yataqay-ya'*

epileptic

مريض بالصرع

mareeD biS-Sara'

asthmatic

مريض بالربو

mareeD bir-rabu

diabetic

مريض بالسكر

mareeD bis-suk-kar

already on antibiotics

يأخذ مضادات حيوية

yaa'khuz muDadaat Hayawey-ya

has an ulcer

عنده قرحة

'andu qurHa

Last year she had...

في العام الماضي...

fil 'aam al-maaDeyy

hepatitis

أصيبت بالصفراء

uSeebat biS-Safraa'

an operation

أجرت جراحة

ajrat jiraaHa

measles

مرضت بالحصبة

mariDat bil-HaSba

Where's the nearest...?

أين أقرب...؟

ain aqrab

pharmacy

صيدلية

Saidaley-ya

bathroom

حمام

Ham-maam

dentist

طبيب أسنان

Tabeeb asnaan

What do you have for...?

ماذا عندك...؟

maadha 'andak

insect bites

للدغ الحشرات

li-ladgh al-Hasharaat

headaches

للصداع

liS-Sudaa'

diarrhea

للإسهال

lil-is-haal

constipation

للإمساك

lil-imsaak

hay fever

لحمى القش

li-Humma l-qash

sunburn

لحروق الشمس

li-Hurooq ash-shams

I can't see anything without my...

أنا لا أرى شيئا دون...

ana laa ara shai'an doon

> glasses
>
> نظارتي
>
> *naDH-DHaaratee*

> contact lenses
>
> عدساتي اللاصقة
>
> *'adasaatee al-laasiqa*

I must protect my eyes.

يجب أن أحمي عيناي.

yajib an aHmee 'ainaaya

Please make sure there's no concussion.

أرجوك تأكد من عدم وجود ارتجاج.

arjook ta'ak-kad min 'adam wujood irtijaaj

Better cover your mouth and nose.

من الأفضل أن تغطي فمك وأنفك.

min al-afDal an tughaT-Tee famak wa anfak

It's one of the allergy symptoms.

هذه واحدة من أعراض الحساسية.

haadhihi waaHida min a'raaD al-Hasaasey-ya

She just fainted suddenly.

أصيبت بالإغماء فجأة.

uSeebat bil-ighmaa' faj'ah

Is the doctor coming now or later?

هل سيأتي الطبيب الآن أم فيما بعد؟

hal saya'tee aT-Tabeeb al-aan am feema ba'd

It's in a very sensitive area.

إنه في منطقة حساسة جدا.

in-nahu fee mantiqa Has-saasa jid-dan

The prescription is not with me right now.

الروشتة ليست معي الآن.

ar-rooshit-ta laisat ma'ee al-aan

Will they allow you to give her a sedative?

هل يسمحون لك أن تعطيها مسكن؟

hal yasmaHoon laki an tu'Teeha musak-kin

Bad Hair Days

diapers	underpants
حفاضات	ملابس داخلية
Haf-faaDat	*malaabis daakhiley-ya*
disinfectant	socks
مطهر	جوارب
muTah-hir	*jawaarib*
tampons	cavity
فوط صحية	تجويف
fuwaT SiH-Hey-ya	*taj-weef*
laxative	toothpaste
ملين	معجون أسنان
mulay-yin	*ma'joon asnaan*
tweezers	eye drops
ملقاط	نقط للعين
milqaaT	*nuqaT lil-'ain*
razors	nose drops
أمواس	نقط للأنف
amwaas	*nuqaT lil-anf*
trash bags	stretcher
أكياس زبالة	نقالة
akiaas zibaala	*naq-qaala*
insect repellent	
طارد للحشرات	
Taarid lil-Hasharaat	

We have to buy an alarm clock.

يجب أن نشتري منبه .

yajib an nashtaree munab-bih

This is my first sandstorm.

هذه أول عاصفة رملية لي .

haadhihi aw-wal 'aaSifa ramley-ya lee

Call an ambulance!

اطلبوا الإسعاف !

uTlubu l-is'aaf

We have to move her to the shade.

يجب أن ننقلها إلى الظل .

yajib an nanqulhaa ila aDH-DHill

I feel sick. Let's go back.

أنا أشعر بالمرض . هيا بنا نرجع .

ana ash'ur bil-maraD. hay-ya bina narja'

I know nothing about treating...

أنا لا أعرف الكثير عن علاج ...

ana la a'rif al-katheer 'an 'ilaaj

> sunstroke
>
> ضربة الشمس
>
> *Darbat ash-shams*

> burns
>
> الحروق
>
> *al-Hurooq*

> dehydration
>
> الجفاف
>
> *aj-jafaaf*

The scorpion bit him right there.

العقرب لدغه هناك .

al-'aqrab ladaghuh hunaak

We have a puncture. Can you help?

عندنا ثقب. ممكن تساعدنا؟

'andana thuqb. mumkin tisaa'idna

I think the injury is serious.

أعتقد أن الإصابة جسيمة.

a'taqid an al-iSaaba jaseema

Don't be offended. We don't know your customs.

لا تغضبوا، نحن لانعرف تقاليدكم.

laa taghDabu, naHnu laa na'rif taqaaleedakum

Long Arm of the Law

We didn't know it was forbidden.

لم نكن نعرف أنه ممنوع.

lam nakun na'rif annu mamnoo'

Tell them to stay away from me.

قل لهم انصرفوا عني.

qul lahum inSarifu 'anni

We are lost.

نحن تهنا.

naHnu tuhna

Are we going to pay a fine?

هل سندفع غرامة؟

hal sa-nadfa' gharaama

Yes, there was a lot of blood.

نعم، كان هناك دم كثير.

na'am, kaan hunaak dam katheer

It was in my handbag when I left the hotel.

كانت في حقيبة يدي حين غادرت الفندق.

kaanat fi Haqeebat yadee Heen ghaadart al-funduq

When the accident happened I was...

حين وقع الحادث أنا كنت...

Heen waqa' al-Haadith ana kunt

asleep

نائم

naa'im

right here

هنا بالضبط

huna biD-Dabt

right there

هناك بالضبط

hunaak biD-Dabt

If I see them I will easily recognize them.

لو رأيتهم سأتعرف عليهم بسهولة.

law ra'aitahum s-'ata'r-raf 'alaihim bi-suhoola

I couldn't see anything because I was...

أنا لم أرى شيئا لأن...

ana lam 'ara shai'an li'an

blinded by the light

الضوء كان في عيني

aD-Daw' kaan fee 'ainee

standing in the dark

كنت أقف في الظلام

kunt aqif fiDH-DHalaam

Our car is stuck in the sand over there.

سيارتنا غرست في الرمال هناك.

say-yaaratna gharasat fir-rimaal hunaak

May I call our consulate in...

ممكن أتصل بقنصليتنا في...

mumkin at-taSil bi-qunSuley-yatna fee

I was swimming and she was reading on the beach.

أنا كنت أسبح وهي كانت تقرأ على الشاطئ.

*ana kunt asbaH wa hiya kaanat taqra'
'ala sh-shaaTi'*

He started harassing me this morning.

بدأ يضايقني هذا الصباح.

bada' yuDaayiqnee haadha S-SabaaH

Stop following me or I'll scream.

كفوا عن تتبعي وإلا صرخت.

kuf-fu 'an tatabu'ee wa'illa Sarakht

He was wearing the traditional clothes.

كان يرتدي الملابس التقليدية.

kaan yartadi al-malaabis at-taqleedey-ya

This boy is a liar.

هذا الولد كاذب.

haadha al-walad kaadhib

He was driving and talking on his cell phone.

كان يقود السيارة وهو يتكلم في الهاتف.

*kaan yaqood as-say-yaara wa huwa yatakal-lam
fil-haatif*

REFERENCE

Numbers

one واحد *waaHid*	ten عشرة *'ashara*
two اثنين *ithnain*	eleven احداعشر *Hidaashar*
three ثلاثة *thalaatha*	twelve اثناعشر *ithnaashar*
four أربعة *arba'a*	thirteen ثلاثة عشر *thalaath t'ashar*
five خمسة *khamsa*	fourteen أربعة عشر *arba'a t'ashar*
six ستة *sit-ta*	fifteen خمسة عشر *khamas t'ashar*
seven سبعة *sab'a*	sixteen ستة عشر *sit-ta t'ashar*
eight ثمانية *thamanya*	seventeen سبعة عشر *sab'a t'ashar*
nine تسعة *tis'a*	eighteen ثمانية عشر *thamanya t'ashar*

nineteen	eighty
تسعة عشر	ثمانين
tis's t'ashar	*thamaaneen*
twenty	ninety
عشرين	تسعين
'ishreen	*tis'een*
twenty-one	a hundred
واحد وعشرين	مية
waaHid wa-'ishreen	*miy-ya*
twenty-two	hundred and one
ستة وعشرين	مية وواحد
ithnain wa-'ishreen	*miy-ya we-waaHid*
twenty-three	hundred and forty
سبعة وعشرين	مية وأربعين
thalaatha wa-'ishreen	*miy-ya wa-arba'een*
thirty	three hundred
ثلاثين	ثلاث مية
thalaatheen	*thalaath miy-ya*
forty	a thousand
أربعين	ألف
arba'een	*alf*
fifty	ten thousand
خمسين	عشرة آلاف
khamseen	*'ashara aalaaf*
sixty	ninety thousand
ستين	تسعين ألف
sit-teen	*tes'een alf*
seventy	a million
سبعين	مليون
saba'een	*milyoon*

Ordinals

first
أول
awall

second
ثان
'thaani

third
ثالث
thaalith

fourth
رابع
raabi'

fifth
خامس
khaamis

sixth
سادس
saadis

seventh
سابع
saabi'

eighth
ثامن
thaamin

ninth
تاسع
taasi'

tenth
عاشر
'aashir

Days of the Week

Monday
الأثنين
al-ithnain

Tuesday
الثلاثاء
ath-thulathaa'

Wednesday
الأربعاء
al-arba'a'

Thursday
الخميس
al-khamees

Friday
الجمعة
aj-jum'a

Saturday
السبت
as-sabt

Sunday
الأحد
al-aHad

Times of the Day

What's the time?
كم الساعة؟
kam as-saa'a

twelve o'clock
الساعة اثناشر
as-saa'a ithnaashar

five past one

واحدة وخمسة

waHda wa-khamsa

ten past two

اثنين وعشرة

ithnain wa-ashra

quarter past three

ثلاثة وربع

thalatha wa-rub'

twenty past four

أربعة وثلث

arba' wa-thulth

twenty-five past six

ستة وخمسة وعشرين

sit-ta wa-khamsa wa-'ishreen

half past seven

سبعة ونصف

saba'a wa-niSf

twenty to eight

ثمانية إلا ثلث

thamanya illa thulth

quarter to nine

تسعة إلا الربع

tis'a illa rub'

ten to ten

عشرة إلا عشرة

'ashra illa 'ashra

five to eleven

حداعشر إلا خمسة